God's Perfect View

20 Stories of Faith and Hope here on Earth

Andrew McCrea

Blake & King

Maysville, Missouri

Published by Blake & King
5650 Berlin Road
Maysville, MO 64469

Publisher's Cataloging-in-Publication Data
McCrea, Andrew.

God's perfect view : 20 stories of faith and hope here on earth – Maysville, MO : Blake & King, 2006.

p. ; cm.
ISBN: 0-9725331-3-3
ISBN13: 978-0-09725331-3-3

1. Christian life. 2. Faith. 3. Hope-Religious aspects-Christianity. I. Title.

BV4495 .M33 2005
248-dc22 2005936221

Book production and coordination by Jenkins Group, Inc. •
www.bookpublishing.com

Interior design by Debbie Sidman
Cover design by Chris Rhoads

Printed in the United States of America

10 09 08 07 06 • 5 4 3 2 1

Dedication

To Florence Wheatley and Jo Blair, my Sunday School teachers, and to all those who have guided me as a Christian.

Contents

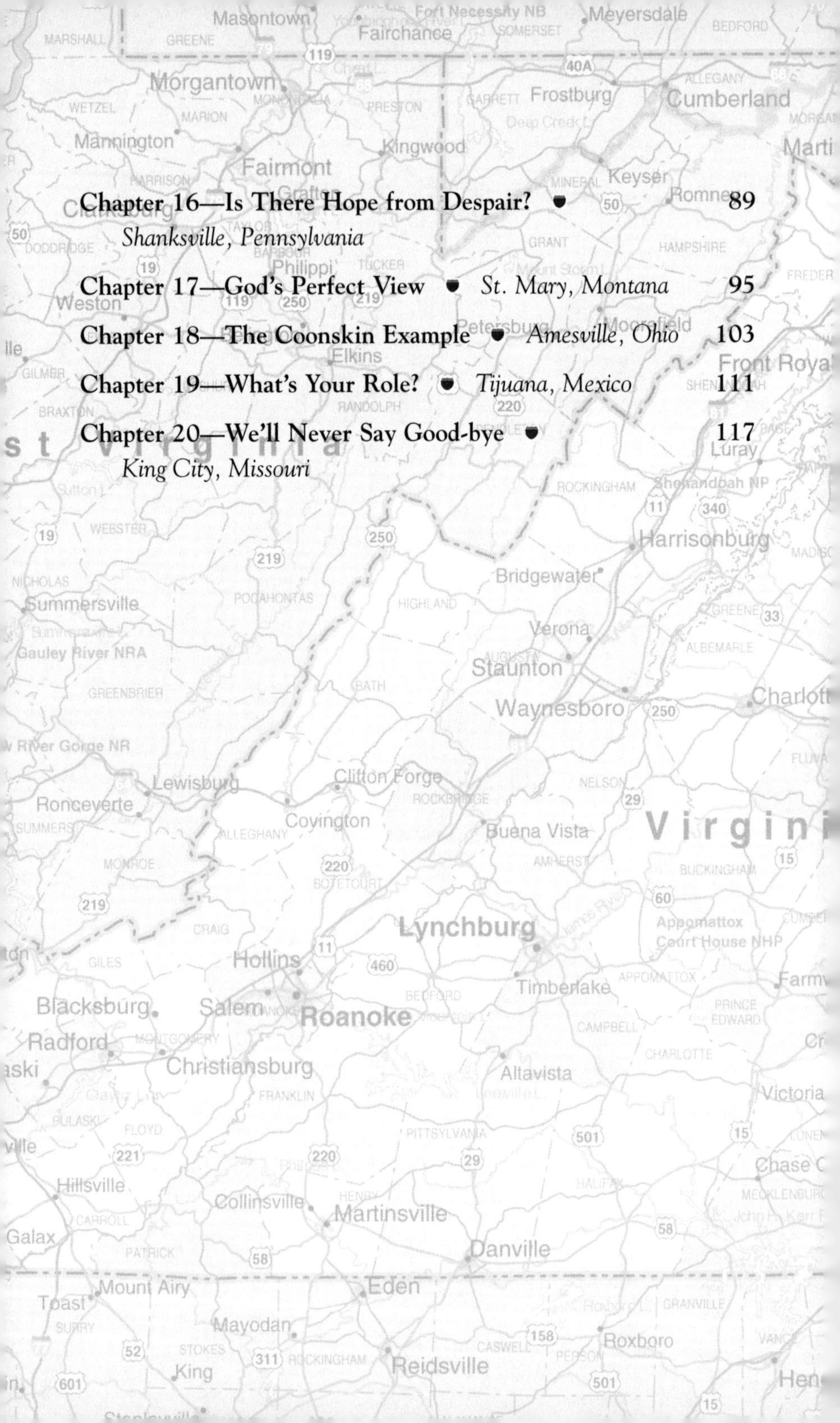
Masontown
Fairchance
Meyersdale
Morgantown
Frostburg
Cumberland
Mannington
Kingwood
Fairmont
Keyser
Philippi
Weston
Elkins
Front Royal
Luray
Shenandoah NP
Harrisonburg
Bridgewater
Summersville
Gauley River NRA
Verona
Staunton
Waynesboro
Lewisburg
Ronceverte
Clifton Forge
Covington
Buena Vista
Virgini
Lynchburg
Appomattox Court House NHP
Hollins
Timberlake
Blacksburg
Salem
Roanoke
Radford
Christiansburg
Altavista
Victoria
Hillsville
Collinsville
Martinsville
Galax
Danville
Mount Airy
Eden
Toast
Mayodan
Roxboro
King
Reidsville

Preface

Faith has always been important to me. From elementary and junior high school on, I played an active role in many church-related activities. I have always been fortunate to have good Christian people in my life who, then and now, inspire me to learn and grow.

Today, I often serve as a lay speaker and teacher and speak on topics of faith to a variety of churches and religious organizations, including many Protestant and Catholic churches. I enjoy this interdenominational approach and have learned much from the experiences.

My background includes both formal and informal education about the Bible. I have earned seminary credit plus attended many classes for church laity. However, it may be my daily radio broadcast, *The American Countryside*, that has provided the most education about my "living" faith. This informal education from interviewing others has been extremely valuable, for I am always inspired to learn how others put their faith into practice.

The first two books that grew out of *The American Countryside* series, *Where Does Lost Luggage Go?* and *The Man Who Was President for a Day*, relate inspirational stories about life and leadership.

While this book does the same, it is devoted exclusively to stories about faith. Written in the same style as the other books, its purpose is to convey stories of faith and hope that will help others grow in their spiritual lives.

I hope you enjoy, learn, and grow as you read *God's Perfect View*.

Chapter 1

Foundations—The Journey Begins

King City, Missouri

For no one can lay any foundation other than the one already laid, which is Jesus Christ.

—I Corinthians 3:11

Beginnings aren't sometimes beginnings at all…at least at the time we live them. We often have no idea we are entering a new phase in life, an important change that will influence our direction forever. It is perhaps only after months or years that we look back and see that one particular moment signaled a beginning. That is the case for a wonderful beginning that took place for me when I was only six years old.

Our church was growing, and we were simply running out of room. It wasn't so much that there was a huge rush of new people coming through the doors, but more that the building was small. My little Sunday school class met in the church kitchen for a while, but with so many people in such a small place, a better alternative was needed.

If we wanted a new and more private place to meet inside the old church building, it would have to be in the basement, and that was a scary proposition. The building was old, and the foundations of the church had been poured without considering that the basement might ever be used for meeting or working space.

It was dark down there too, especially to a six-year-old. I was afraid to venture very far from the set of stairs that led downward, as it seemed one might vanish into a great dark abyss. The stairs themselves were scary, as one could only go down them by lifting a trap door. That door had to be shut when services were held in the main sanctuary, or else the minister might back up too far from the pulpit and fall in!

People did go down to part of the basement regularly for storage, and occasionally the trap door was accidentally closed with someone still below. Usually, just before the main worship service began, you could hear someone banging on the door wishing to be let out.

I imagined that if I ever went down there, I might be locked in and not rescued until the following Sunday.

In spite of my fear, this was where we had to go if our little Sunday school class wanted a place to meet, and we had just the person to lead us on such an expedition. God had given Jo Blair the talents needed to lead a group of first graders on such a mission. She was unbelievably positive, and if she had doubts, she didn't let us see them. She was fun, and she cared about each one of us as much as she did her own family.

We quickly learned that if we wanted to make ourselves a classroom in the church basement, it would have to be at the very back of the basement, and that was the scariest part of all. There was only one window in the whole basement, at the front end, of course. Other classes had already taken the front, and there weren't even lights in the portion we were allotted, as if the electricians had known that area would never be utilized.

The day finally came for Jo to lead us on our first great journey into that unexplored space, and it was then that we learned why this portion of the building had never been used. While the ceiling above our heads, the church's main floor, remained at a constant level, the cement floor beneath us had a unique feature…it steadily rose the further one walked into the basement.

This proved to be no problem at the front of the basement where the door was located, as the height there was about eight feet. But as one kept walking, the floor moved closer to the ceiling, until at the very back the distance had shrunk to about five feet. I was only six, so this was not a problem for me, but most adults couldn't avoid banging their heads unless they were very careful.

My classmate Brett and I were the only ones accompanying Jo on her first adventure into the basement. I remember stopping and staring at the area she selected for our little group to meet. It was dark and dusty and appeared not to have been used for anything except storage.

Brett saw the good in the place and piped up, "I think it will work just great, Jo." With that he leaned a hand on one of the green steel poles supporting the floor above. The pole fell over with a metal clanking that reverberated throughout the dimly lit space.

We all laughed, and Jo said, "Brett, I hope you don't cause the church to fall in on us before we even meet down here!"

One other unique feature of that basement was the walls. Since the foundation of the church had not been poured with the idea of using the basement, little care had been taken to make the cement sides smooth. They were jagged, with cement chunks protruding several inches from the sides. The mass of cement also widened as it approached the floor, making the walls look more like steep cement mountains than smooth basement walls.

Jo saw those walls as an opportunity. By the next Sunday, she had put up curtains to make our area feel more like a room, and she had painted the wall light green for the first four feet and light blue the rest of the way up. She told us this would be our Bible story wall, and over the following years, we took great care and time to construct scenes from the Bible on what was once a very ugly wall.

The wall jutted out so much that we were able to build a Noah's ark and place it on the wall, along with animals walking two by two down the side to the floor as they came out of the giant boat after the flood. In another area, Lazarus, still bound in grave clothes, had been raised from the dead by Jesus and stood outside his tomb.

Seeing those stories come to life on that wall and hearing the passion with which Jo Blair shared them stuck with me forever. **The literal foundation of the church became the foundation for my life.**

Eventually, the church built permanent wooden walls to cover the cement ones and make the basement more attractive. They left a tiny crawl space though, and on one occasion I squeezed back there to look at the old green and blue wall that had once been part of my Sunday School classroom.

Years later, my small town church closed. There just weren't enough parishioners to justify the place remaining open. The day we sang our last hymn and said goodbye to the church was the only day I ever cried in public.

I purchased the old hymn board from the church, and I've always left the final hymn number on it as a reminder of God's call for my life. It's hymn number 502, "I'll Go Where You Want Me to Go." The last verse sung that day says,

There's surely somewhere a lowly place in earth's harvest fields so wide
where I may labor thru life's short day for Jesus the Crucified.
So, trusting my all unto Thy care I know Thou lovest me
I'll do Thy will with a heart sincere, I'll be what You want me to be.

Chorus:
I'll go where You want me to go, dear Lord, O'er mountain or plain or sea;
I'll say what you want me to say, dear Lord, I'll be what You want me to be.

Whenever I find myself in a tough situation in life, I find myself singing those words. I Corinthians 3:11 says, "For no one can lay any foundation other than the one already laid, which is Jesus Christ." I have realized just how important that foundation is.

That is why this book is about foundations...it is about building a Christian foundation that will stand for eternity.

My grandfather McCrea used to tell a story about his great-grandfather attending church in what is now the ghost town of Winslow, Missouri. My great-great-great-grandfather was a leader in the church and was in his nineties when this story takes place. He had lost most of his hearing at this point, but my grandfather recalled him saying most of the prayers in church.

Because the old gentleman was hard of hearing, the parishioners had worked out a signal to indicate to him when it was time for him to pray. They would simply turn and look at him and nod their heads as if to say, "It's time for you to pray now." He would then launch into prayer in his southern drawl, always concluding with, "In the name of our great redeemer, Amen."

This prayer cue worked great unless someone unintentionally looked at him too long. Unable to hear what was taking place around him, my great-great-great-grandfather would mistakenly believe this was his signal to begin, and would stop the proceedings with one of his invocations in the name of "the great redeemer."

I always like to share this story when I go to a new church to speak or deliver a message. In addition to farming, I'm a certified lay pastor, which means I fill in at churches as needed and do a variety of other teaching and speaking work for churches. I also produce a daily radio feature and enjoy speaking to many groups each year. I especially enjoy speaking at various denominations of Protestant and Catholic churches. Each seems to have a slightly different method of conducting services. That causes me, like my great-great-great-grandfather, to look around for my cues, to make sure I don't do something "wrong."

These travels have taught me a lot about the wonderful foundation Christians share in Jesus Christ. Yes, there are differences in how we worship and how we interpret specific portions of the Bible. The first disciples disagreed on some of those things too, but they still served the same God and sought to worship in harmony with one another.

I often reflect on the words in the chorus of the final hymn we sang that last Sunday at my hometown church: "I will go where you want me to go, dear Lord." I simply like to share words from the Bible, foundations taught to me by people like Jo Blair, that have guided me for life.

You will find that the point, or moral, of each chapter in this book is included in a shaded box with a compass symbol. The first compasses were used by the Chinese almost two thousand years ago. They used lodestones, a mineral composed of iron oxide, that aligns itself in a north-south direction. These natural magnets were eventually placed on squares with directional markings. Once navigators found north, they immediately knew how to find east, south, and west.

Jesus spoke about the importance of our life's foundation. In Luke 6:47-49 he said, "I will show you what he is like who comes to me and hears my words and puts them into practice. He is like a man building a house, who dug down deep and laid the foundation on rock. When a flood came, the torrent struck that house but could not shake it, because it was well built. But the one who hears my words and does not put them into practice is like a man who built a house on the ground without a foundation. The moment the torrent struck that house, it collapsed and its destruction was complete." We should build our lives just as we build a house, beginning with the foundation.

The shaded boxes in this book work much the same as a compass. These simple points are designed to give our lives direction. As we begin to apply these lessons to our lives, we are better able to navigate the challenges we encounter every day. These boxes are part of the stories they appear in, yet they are highlighted to emphasize the "direction" they can provide us.

This book, *God's Perfect View*, is designed to give us perspectives on living with powerful faith. Maybe you have never built such a foundation, or perhaps you have built on the wrong foundation. Maybe Jesus isn't the cornerstone of your life. Perhaps you are familiar with some of the Bible stories or have even gone to church a few times, but haven't found it to your liking. Maybe you even wonder why this particular foundation is important.

Perhaps you have a foundation, but have failed to do much construction on it. Maybe you are busy with other things or feel working on this foundation just doesn't matter anymore.

Whatever your situation, I believe you will find points in this book that will guide you in your task. As you read these stories, you may find that they hold a slightly different application for you than they do for me. Great! As Jesus shared his parables, he knew each story held an important truth, yet the hearer might apply that truth to a different area of his or her life. Each of us has our own hurdles, and each story that follows can give us help in meeting our particular challenges. That's what makes the words of the Bible timeless, for the words continue to apply to our lives today.

I also encourage you to pick up a Bible and read beyond what is presented here. Hopefully, I've included verses that inspire you to learn more. This book is designed to help each one of us desire to dig deeper and live stronger. It is written so that each of us may build upon a strong foundation that will stand for eternity.

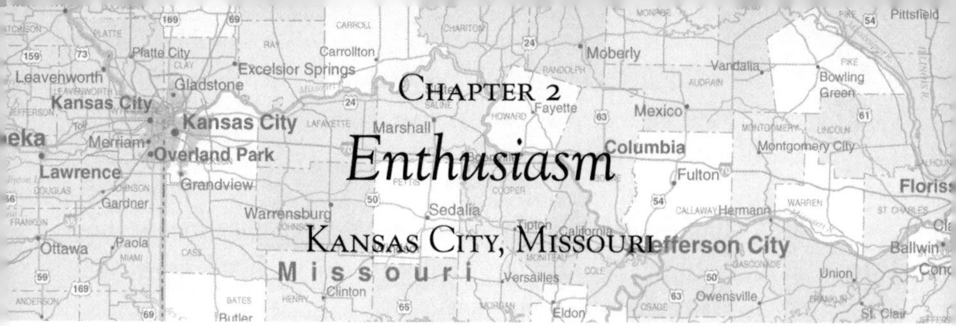

CHAPTER 2

Enthusiasm

KANSAS CITY, MISSOURI

About midnight Paul and Silas were praying and singing hymns to God, and the other prisoners were listening to them.

—ACTS 16:25

Team mascots at sporting events may not play the game, yet many of us believe they play a vital role in its outcome. I have always been a big Kansas City Royals baseball fan. When I can't be at a game, I usually try to watch it on TV or listen on the radio. The Royals, like many other baseball teams, have a mascot. Theirs is a lion named Sluggerrr, and he does his fair share of hugging kids and cheering on the team through a variety of antics.

As the Royals slogged their way through the rest of their schedule in 2004, up until then the worst season in the club's history, I listened to them blow yet another lead and lose the game in extra innings. I decided to listen to the barrage of callers berating the team during the post-game call-in show. After an hour of listening to everyone's ideas of how to fix the team, the host announced he would take just one more call.

A man named Frank came on the line and stated, "I'm really upset tonight. I'm upset with the team, but I'm even more upset with someone in the stands."

"How can you be upset with someone in the stands?" the host asked.

"Well, all of us fans were doing our best to keep cheering on the team in extra innings, but we just can't do it alone," Frank growled.

"So…you need *who* to help you?"

"I looked all over the stadium, and I couldn't find Sluggerrr anywhere! Where was he? That's his job; he's supposed to lead us in cheering on the team!"

There was a long pause from the host as Frank's anger toward the team's lion-headed mascot came to a boil.

"Well, well, well…it's come to this, hasn't it?" The host seemingly shook his head in disbelief to those few still tuned in to hear that night's debacle on the diamond. "We are now blaming a *mascot* for our losses…a *mascot* for crying out loud…a *mascot* who never bats or fields or does anything but kiss kids and shoot hot dogs with a super-sized hot dog gun. If the *mascot* is the source of our problems, there's no way this call-in show is going to help us. That's it. Good night. We'll try and win one tomorrow."

It seems silly to try to pin a baseball team's loss on the absence of a mascot, but think about it. As human beings, we place a lot of importance on the cheers of the crowd. After all, why is there such a thing as home field advantage? Why do odds-makers give teams an advantage when they play on their own court? Nothing about the field, court, or the players changes…only the surroundings change. The enthusiasm of the crowd is counted as an advantage to the home team.

What does such enthusiasm look like in the Bible? Paul and Silas are ambassadors for Christ as they crisscross the Roman Empire delivering the news of Jesus, proclaiming him as Savior. This wasn't a popular message, and it probably seemed as if the two would never get to hear the cheering crowds that welcome a home team when they take to the field. Yet this pair certainly lived with enthusiasm for Christ.

In Acts 16:21, Paul and Silas aren't about to find any cheering hoard to bolster their message. In fact, they are soon thrown into prison in Philippi because, in the words of their accusers, they are "teaching customs which are not lawful for us to receive, neither observe, being Romans." The crowd is so incensed with these men that they tear off their clothes, beat them, and throw them into the stocks in the inner portion of the prison.

Think for a moment about the men already in prison who have just watched this series of events unfold. Word travels fast, and they probably know what Paul and Silas have done to earn their tough treatment. They've been chirping about Jesus, and now it's going to cost them. They might be thinking, "Let's see how much talking these guys want to do now."

What do Paul and Silas do? "About midnight Paul and Silas were praying and singing hymns to God, and the other prisoners were listening to them" (Acts 16:25). These men who have just been tortured for the words they've spoken are now singing praises to God...they are repeating the very acts that got them thrown into prison in the first place.

What do the other prisoners think of this? I've wondered if those prisoners yelled down to them, "Knock it off...we're trying to sleep!" We don't know if anything was said, but we do know the prisoners were listening. They were listening to what was taking place, and what they heard had an effect on them.

In my travels as a journalist I once visited Alcatraz, the maximum-security prisoner on an island in San Francisco Bay. To see the prison you wear a headset, which provides an audio tour of the facility and broadcasts interviews with former prisoners. These interviews describe what conditions and everyday life were like inside the walls, and they provide fascinating insights as you walk along the rows of cells.

I specifically remember the words of one of those prisoners. He recalled one New Year's Eve in the prison, and as he lay in his cell trying to sleep, he could hear the celebration taking place across the water along the San Francisco wharf. The heavy fog that often hovers just above the water helped carry the sound across the great distance between the shore and the island referred to as "The Rock." On this New Year's Eve, this prisoner could actually make out conversations. He could hear women laughing. He heard singing. He ended his description with the words "...and I wished I was there."

The prisoner was listening. Isn't it interesting what we hear in our quiet times, times when we are or feel totally alone? The prisoners listened to Paul and Silas. The jailor listened to Paul and Silas. What they heard had an effect on them.

Before we go further, something else should be said about Paul and Silas' singing. We don't know if those two were really that great of a duet. For some reason, I don't get the feeling they had the talent to take their act on the road. I don't know that the quality of their singing was that special, but the quantity of their singing and the joy with which they sang was.

Men, and in some cases women, don't often sing like they used to. I think the reason is that we are afraid we don't sound very good and that others will be annoyed if we sing too loudly.

I was once conducting a radio interview in Montana with a Lewis and Clark historian. One of this gentleman's particular interests was music, so we discussed the expedition and the singing and dancing the men engaged in on their two-and-a-half year trip in 1804-1806. At one point I asked, "So when did they sing? Did they have a set time in the evening when someone would begin singing?"

Frustrated, the historian said to me, "No, no...you just don't understand. This is not like today, when guys say, 'Sing? No...my wife sings, but not me...I'm no good.' Singing was a guy thing. They sang all the time, in happy times and in sad times. It was part of their life."

I've attended men's retreats where the singing nearly blew the roof off the building. It is amazing what happens when there are just guys in the room and they know no one else can hear them. They belt out some of the loudest and most joyful singing you will ever hear. But put them in church or any other public gathering and they typically find a singing voice slightly louder than a whisper. We shouldn't worry about how we sound. God says to make a joyful "noise," and we need to make one!

So here are Paul and Silas, praying and belting out hymns at midnight, when suddenly an earthquake opens all the prison doors. When the head jailor sees what has happened, he is ready to kill himself because he knows all the prisoners in his charge will have escaped. Just when he is ready to end it all, Paul and Silas spring in and cry out, "Don't harm yourself! We are all here!" (Acts 16:28).

Everyone stays! Think about it. The two guys who were just beaten up and have every reason to run away as fast as they can stick around...and not only that, they influence everyone else to stay, too!

The events of the past few hours have had an effect. As Paul and Silas come to the jailor, he asks them, "What must I do to be saved?" He has been listening. The prisoners have been listening. All of them have heard the message.

How could Paul and Silas sing in the middle of the night after enduring so much hardship? They could sing because they knew they had everything they could ever want. They had Jesus. They knew that men could beat them and take everything they had except their faith. They responded to the jailor's question with these words: "Believe in the Lord Jesus, and you will be saved" (Acts 16:31).

In the next chapter we'll talk more about the message Paul and Silas had for the jailer, but the important point for now is to recognize the effect these two men had on the entire prison just by singing and praying. Paul and Silas were on their way to converting the entire prison, and they influenced criminals not to run when the cell doors opened and set them free.

But you see, it wasn't the cell doors that set them free. It was the words of Jesus that set them free forever. It was the faith Paul and Silas shared with the prisoners that set them free for eternity.

If you don't think Paul and Silas' enthusiasm was a big deal, just think about what would have happened if they had been thrown into jail and done nothing. If no prayer had been said nor any hymn sung, if there had been nothing for the prisoners and jailor to hear, there would have been no need for God to send an earthquake. There would have been no reason to set Paul and Silas free. With that much enthusiasm for the faith they possessed, no prison could hold them, for no one could resist the message they shared. Enthusiasm for the faith we possess transforms our lives and the lives of those around us!

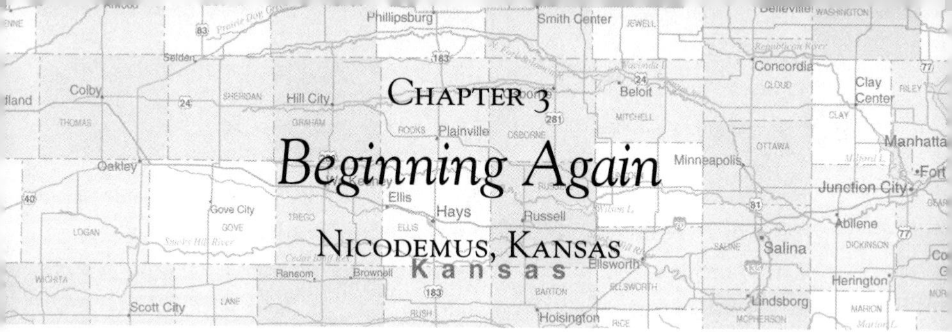

CHAPTER 3

Beginning Again

NICODEMUS, KANSAS

Jesus declared, "I tell you the truth, no one can see the kingdom of God unless he is born again." "How can a man be born when he is old?" Nicodemus asked. "Surely he cannot enter a second time into his mother's womb to be born!"

—JOHN 3:3-4

In the years following the Civil War, African Americans struggled to take full advantage of the new freedoms afforded them. Grievous oppression still existed in many areas, and groups such as the Ku Klux Klan intimidated and even killed black citizens. Customs and deliberate laws combined to make it difficult for former slaves to buy land or find good jobs. These factors, along with a lack of education, often produced a form of economic slavery in the south.

In 1877, as the federal government began to withdraw troops from the south after Reconstruction, conditions further deteriorated and many blacks looked to leave the south and begin life anew in other areas of the country. One of the men who helped organize groups to move from the south was Henry Adams. The disparaging conditions blacks endured were captured in a petition Adams wrote, a petition that was signed by nearly 100,000 people and sent to President Rutherford Hayes. It reads:

> If that protection cannot be given and our [Constitutional] rights [cannot be] restored, we would respectfully ask that some Territory be assigned to us in which we can colonize our race; and if that cannot be done, to appropriate means so that we can colonize in Liberia or some other country, for we feel and know that unless full and ample protection is guaranteed to us we cannot live in the South, and will and must colonize under some other government, and we put our full trust in God that our prayers and petition will be speedily answered.

The president never responded to the petition, but this document shows the desire of African Americans to take full advantage of the freedoms they were supposed to have.

Another such effort to improve life for blacks began when W. R. Hill and Reverend W. H. Smith formed the Nicodemus Town Company. Two towns in Graham County, Kansas, were platted. Hill City was a white community named for Hill himself, and Nicodemus was a town for blacks, named for a legendary slave who purchased his freedom. A spiritual song of the time proclaimed the following:

Nicodemus was a slave of African birth,
And was bought for a bag full of gold;
He was reckoned a part of the salt of the earth,
But he died years ago, very old.
Nicodemus was a prophet, at least he was as wise,
For he told of battles to come;
How we trembled with fear, when he rolled up his eyes,
And we heeded the shake of his thumb.

Chorus:
Good time coming, good time coming,
Long, long time on the way;

Run and tell Elija to hurry up Pomp,
To meet us under the cottonwood tree,
In the Great Solomon Valley.

At its height, the town of Nicodemus numbered about 800 people. Today it is just a small town along U.S. 24 in western Kansas, but the impact this place made looms large in the history of the United States. A few descendents of those original settlers still call Nicodemus home, and this community remains a legacy of the struggle former slaves undertook in order to experience true freedom and the opportunity for a new life.

John Solomon Lewis, one of the early residents, summed up what it meant to live there when he said, "When I landed on the soil, I looked on the ground and I says this is free ground. Then I looked on the heavens, and I says them is free and beautiful heavens. Then I looked within my heart, and I says to myself I wonder why I never was free before?"

Lewis' words hold deep meaning: "...I wonder why I never was free before?" They speak of the joy the settlers of Nicodemus felt to be free and to have a place of their own to live, despite the struggles of living on the desolate plains.

In the Bible, it is a man named Nicodemus rather than a town that is at the center of a discussion about becoming "free." It is a visit with Jesus that produces much the same effect, an opportunity to begin a new life.

Becoming "free" or becoming a "new man" is a concept we find repeatedly in the Bible. In fact, it was Nicodemus who asked Jesus about becoming a "new man" in a sense. In John 3:3-4 Jesus declared, "I tell you the truth, no one can see the kingdom of God unless he is born again."

"How can a man be born when he is old?" Nicodemus asked. "Surely he cannot enter a second time into his mother's womb to be born!"

The Greek word for "again" can be translated as "above." In other words, Jesus is telling Nicodemus he needs to be "born from above."

Jesus speaks directly to Nicodemus about what it means to be born from above. In John 3:16-18 he continues, "For God so loved the world that he gave his one and only Son, that whoever believes in him shall not perish but have eternal life. For God did not send his Son into the world to condemn the world, but to save the world through him. Whoever believes in him is not condemned, but whoever does not believe stands condemned already because he has not believed in the name of God's one and only Son."

We are born physically into this world as sinners. Yet Christ proclaims that those who experience that birth from above are free from the bondage of sin and now seek to serve Him.

In some ways, this reminds me of those early residents of Nicodemus, Kansas. They desired to be free, and that desire led them to begin again in a new town. When we are born from above, we also seek to be free from sin to serve God. We believe in him as our Savior and make a commitment to follow him.

Let me pause for a moment to discuss this commitment. Remember that in the Bible, people express this commitment, being "born from above," in differing ways. Paul has a dramatic conversion on the road to Damascus and he then begins serving God. The Ethiopian in Acts 8 needs someone to help teach him what the scriptures say, and then he makes a commitment to follow Christ. Timothy is raised in a Christian home and probably never knows anything but to be committed to serving God.

These three examples show that the Holy Spirit works in people's hearts in different ways, but in every case, the person steps out to make a commitment to follow Christ, in effect saying, "I choose to be 'born from above.'"

Consider the scene at the cross as Jesus is crucified with a thief on either side of him. Luke 23:39-43 records the discussion these three men have as they await physical death: "One of the criminals who hung there hurled insults at him: 'Aren't you the Christ? Save yourself and us!'

"But the other criminal rebuked him. 'Don't you fear God,' he said, 'since you are under the same sentence? We are punished justly, for we are getting what our deeds deserve. But this man has done nothing wrong.'

"Then he said, 'Jesus, remember me when you come into your kingdom.'

"Jesus answered him, 'I tell you the truth, today you will be with me in paradise.'"

One thief doesn't believe Jesus is anyone special. He taunts him to the end. The other thief realizes what is taking place. He knows that Jesus is a sinless man who allows himself to die in order to take all the sins of the world upon himself. This thief knows that he justly deserves to be put to death for the crime he has committed, and he recognizes Jesus is the Savior who can save him from his sins. To him, Jesus is exactly who he claims to be in his conversation with Nicodemus: he is the man who offers eternal life in heaven. For the thief, his commitment to Christ comes while hanging on the cross.

Baptism is a sign of that commitment. The Ethiopian in Acts asks to be baptized immediately as a sign of his new life. Some Christians dip their fingers in holy water and make the sign of the cross every time they enter church. This is more than a tradition; it is a way of remembering their baptism and the price Christ paid on the cross for their salvation. We also remember that commitment through the sharing of the Lord's Supper through Eucharist or Communion.

Those who are born from above should also pray about how to spread the message that Jesus shares with Nicodemus. This begins with the lives we lead. Saint Francis of Assisi said, "Spread the gospel, sometimes use words." This is very important. If I say I am a follower of Christ yet my life doesn't reflect what it means to be a Christian, I doubt I will have much influence on people.

Jesus' message involves us being ready to share through words as well. Many of us believe that since we are not gifted evangelists, we lack the skills to speak with others on the subject, or that doing so will make people mad and completely alienate us from most of society. Therefore, we typically decide not to share this very important part of our lives, but you may be surprised at how such messages can affect people.

Before the use of e-mail, I used to send and receive letters from people of all ages, many of whom I'd met at speaking engagements. A couple of friends of mine did this as well. Although the topics of our letters were often about the conferences we had spoken at, we often placed a Bible verse at the bottom of each letter. I wouldn't write the verse out, but would simply write down the reference, such as "Mark 8:36." This act was unobtrusive, yet a way someone might know that faith was an important part of my life, and it might begin a discussion about faith or the Bible. I originally got the idea from a major league baseball player who signed autographs with a scripture notation underneath his name.

While working at a very large youth convention, I remember hearing a speaker briefly mention faith. This was not a church conference, so the topic of the speech was not faith, but the speaker said something like, "Faith in God gives me strength in my life." That was about all that was said on the topic, yet those words triggered a reaction.

One young lady in the audience went to a friend of mine and asked if she could meet the speaker. She said, "I've read some of the verses at the bottom of your letters to me. Now the speaker has mentioned faith, and all I know is that I want to go talk to him about it."

People hear, learn, and accept Christ's message in many different ways. Just be open to sharing. God will open doors and hearts to that message. Keep living a life that is an example of the message Christ shared, but also be ready to speak about why you live the life you do.

If you are "born from above," remember that the life you live should reflect the new man or woman you have become. It is distressing to hear someone say, "I'm already a believer, so I can do what I want; Jesus will forgive me." Yes, Jesus does say salvation comes through faith, but our new lives should reflect that faith. We'll discuss that topic more in the next chapter.

Paul urges Christians in the book of Romans to share their stories with others. In Romans 10:14-15 he writes, "...how can they believe in the one of whom they have not heard? And how can they hear without someone preaching to them? And how can they preach unless they are sent?"

People cannot believe in a message they've never heard. Pray about how God wants you to share. God knows you, and he can use your unique life experiences to reach others. Consider the words of Christ to Nicodemus, "You must be born from above." These are words each of us should reflect upon as we live our lives.

Chapter 4

Freedom

Denali National Park, Alaska

The woman said to the serpent, "We may eat fruit from the trees in the garden, but God did say, 'You must not eat fruit from the tree that is in the middle of the garden, and you must not touch it, or you will die.'"

"You will not surely die," the serpent said to the woman. "For God knows that when you eat of it your eyes will be opened, and you will be like God, knowing good and evil."

—Genesis 3:2-5

Denali National Park offers some of the most beautiful scenery you will find anywhere in the nation. Nestled in the center of Alaska with Mt. McKinley rising into the sky, the natural beauty and abundant wildlife are truly something everyone should see.

If you've ever been camping in bear country like Denali, you know that bears have a very good sense of smell. At night, you have to scour your campsite to make sure all food items have been placed in airtight containers. You then take those containers and hoist them high in the air, using a couple of trees for your poles. The technique hopefully keeps bears from getting to your food, even if they should somehow get a whiff of it. Otherwise, you might easily have a bear rummaging through your campsite at night looking for something to eat.

At the heart of Denali is a bakery that serves the many tourists and overnight campers in the area, and the story is told of a hungry bear who once wanted too much of a good thing. Although precautions were taken to keep bears out of the area, one bear picked up the scent of the tantalizing food and decided he wanted to be a customer, too. Soon the bear was tromping around the building looking for a way to squeeze inside. Park rangers had to come and shoot him with a tranquilizer gun and move him a few miles away to restore calm and safety.

The next morning, who showed up for breakfast but that same bear! Even though he had been moved several miles away, he knew the path back to the bakery. Once again, the bear was shot and moved even farther away over a mountain range.

A few days later, the bear was back again. He knew exactly where that bakery was, and he just kept coming back. Finally, the bear was tranquilized and transported to the lower 48 states, where he now resides in a zoo for bears. He lost the freedom he once enjoyed because he wouldn't stay away from the bakery.

Interestingly enough, some people believe Christians give up some of their freedoms, too. One might legitimately ask whether God's rules even take a little of the fun out of life. It's a point to consider: why does God have "rules" that we should follow?

Several years ago while attending college, I went to a local church service on a Sunday morning in which the minister told the story of two dogs he had purchased. One was a black dog and the other spotted. Because the minister lived along a busy street on the edge of town, he was afraid his two new dogs might run off and be hit by a car. (There was no leash law in this area.) The minister decided to tie the dogs to a long leash behind the house until they'd learned to stay in his yard.

After a couple of weeks, the minister decided it was time to let the dogs run free in the lawn. That afternoon when he returned home, he found the spotted dog playing in the street. The dog needed to learn that he couldn't run in the street, so the minister got out of his car and chased him back into the yard. He hoped this would teach the dog a lesson. The last thing he wanted was for his new dog to be hit by a car right in front of his home.

The next afternoon the minister returned home to find the same situation: the spotted dog was running in the street while the other dog stayed in the yard. This time the minister was more forceful, yelling at the spotted dog and chasing him out of the street again.

On the third day, the minister returned home and found the exact same situation: the spotted dog was once again playing in the street. The minister knew this could not go on any longer, so he got out the leash and tied the spotted dog in the back yard. Today, the black dog roams around the house and even gets to take trips with the minister, and he has never gone into the street. This dog can be trusted, because even in a new location, he listens to his master and doesn't stray to places he shouldn't go. The spotted dog remains on his leash in the back yard, roaming only as far as the rope will allow. He never gets to leave home.

A Christian's life is similar to the story of the Denali bear and the two dogs. Although I have the freedom of choice in my life, God's word sets guidelines that I should follow, and crossing certain boundaries has consequences. If I follow God's rules I will not swear, I won't get drunk, I won't have unmarried sex, I will be honest and fair in all that I do…in other words, Christians are commanded to do certain things that some might say takes away their freedoms.

If we see clear reasons why specific behaviors can hurt us, we might agree that choosing these behaviors is a bad thing to do, no matter if we are free to do them or not, but what if the consequence are not so clear? We don't have God's perfect view. He can see what we cannot. He knows how our decisions affect our lives, both in the short and long term.

When you remember the two dogs, remember that while the spotted dog had a lot of fun roaming the streets, he was most likely going to be injured or killed by a car someday. That is why God sets up guidelines to keep us from those things that will ultimately harm us.

Let's go back to the very first boundary God puts in place and see how crossing the line has dire consequences. In Genesis 2 and 3, the creation of Adam and Eve and their life in the Garden of Eden is recorded. God tells Adam, "You are free to eat from any tree in the garden; but you must not eat from the tree of the knowledge of good and evil, for when you eat of it you will surely die" (Genesis 2:17).

Most of us know what happens: Adam and Eve, with encouragement from Satan, do the one thing God tells them not to do.

In Genesis 3 we gain insight into how Satan works to get us to cross boundaries that ultimately hurt us and separate us from God. Satan speaks to Eve and questions, "Did God really say, 'You must not eat from any tree in the garden'?" (Genesis 3:1). Eve knows the consequence that God said would come from eating the fruit, but Satan calls into question God's rule. "'You will not surely die,' the serpent said to the woman. 'For God knows that when you eat of it your eyes will be opened, and you will be like God, knowing good and evil'" (Genesis 3:2-5).

This reminds me of the man who buys a fake designer watch from someone on the street. He believes he has gotten a great deal, until his shiny new watch breaks after just a little use. Satan is the great imitator; he tempts us by making us believe we are getting a real deal. It's easy to be tempted when we believe we are getting something that will satisfy our desires and will save us time, money, or work. That's what happens to Adam and Eve: "When the woman saw that the fruit of the tree was good for food and pleasing to the eye, and also desirable for gaining wisdom, she took some and ate it. She also gave some to her husband, who was with her, and he ate it" (Genesis 3:6).

If the fruit had looked rotten and tasted horrible, it would have been no problem to stay away from it. If all the negative choices in life were laced with immediate and terrible consequences one hundred percent of the time, they would be much easier to resist. But of course, Satan doesn't work that way. 2 Corinthians 11:14 reminds us of Satan's methods: "And no wonder, for Satan himself masquerades as an angel of light."

In other words, Satan usually tries to make himself and his temptations look like they are good for us, or at the very least, that they won't harm us. He is an imitator. That's why the fruit looks good. That's why the fruit tastes good. But the fruit has terrible consequences. The rest of Genesis 3 records what happens as a result of Adam and Eve eating the fruit they are told not to consume. Ultimately, the chapter is a record of how sin first enters the world and how all men and women must die physically because of that choice.

I can use deceit to pile up riches, but not know the true joy of friends earned through honesty and character. I can fill my eyes with pornography, but not know what it is like to be truly loved by a spouse. I can fill myself with alcohol or drugs and experience an escape from reality, but find myself with deeper troubles still surrounding me. I can run from God's rules and experience the thrill of "freedom," but miss out on the ultimate freedom that comes from a relationship with God through Christ.

Again and again, Satan seeks to imitate God's perfect plan for our lives, offering a shortcut that leads only to brokenness.

Romans 5:18-19 speaks of the first sin of Adam and Eve and the life that Christ offers: "Consequently, just as the result of one trespass was condemnation for all men, so also the result of one act of righteousness was justification that brings life for all men. For just as through the disobedience of the one man the many were made sinners, so also through the obedience of the one man the many will be made righteous."

The righteousness and obedience of that one man, Christ, is what can erase the condemnation of the sin in our lives that first enters the world through Adam and Eve in the Garden of Eden.

The ultimate joy is to experience eternity with God in heaven. Satan's job is to sell us on the notion that ultimate happiness can be found apart from God, but God's "boundaries" are put in place to help us find ultimate victory and joy in a life lived close to Him. God wants to keep us from those things that he knows will eventually harm us, although Satan, through temptations, tries to persuade us differently.

The next chapter reveals how we can experience tremendous strength in a life lived within God's boundaries, and also how we can suffer when we decide to journey outside those lines.

Chapter 5

Thin Ice

Washington, DC

He awoke from his sleep and thought,
"I'll go out as before and shake myself free."
But he did not know that the LORD had left him.

—Judges 16:20

From the time I was a kid, I can remember having to go out to farm ponds and watering tanks to chop ice in the winter. It's one of the necessities of ranching in order to make sure the stock can get something to drink. I've seen plenty of ice and snow in my lifetime, but for those who live in the deep south of the U.S., such winter elements are much more rare.

I have two good friends, one from Texas and the other from near Phoenix, who are fascinated with snow and ice. They like to see it, play in it, drive in it…All the things northerners hate about it, they like, mostly because they so seldom get to experience it.

So, it's no surprise that while on a business trip to the nation's capital, my friend from Texas was captivated by a sheet of ice covering the long reflecting pool between the Washington Monument and the Lincoln Memorial. It was a warm day in early March, and the sheet of ice that had covered the entire pool was beginning to melt. In fact, one side of the pool was liquid water, but the other side, shaded by a line of trees, was still covered by a thick layer of ice. Indeed, the ice was so thick on that side that about one hundred people were playing and sliding on the icy portion of the reflecting pool.

My friend began heading for that icy sheet. Curt had never been to a place where he could walk on ice before, and he just had to experience it. This was a dream come true for him, and he wasn't about to leave anytime soon.

Before long, Curt was slipping and sliding over the huge expanse of ice. He seemed very interested in just how close he could safely get to the thawed side of the pool. I kept my mouth shut and began walking around the pool to the thawed side toward the street. There was no use telling a grown man about thin ice. No matter that he was from the south, he was old enough to know better. Soon it was a competition for him to venture farther to the thawed side than anyone else. After a few careful steps, he'd accomplished it…he'd ventured the farthest onto the thin ice!

At this moment, a question I had long wondered was quickly answered: "Just how deep is that reflecting pool?"

Curt fell in three feet deep as the thin ice cracked and gave way under his feet. There was nothing to do but splash his way out, making tall strides like a high hurdler in slow motion as he lunged for the sidewalk surrounding the pool.

What struck me as I walked was how clearly I could see what was going to happen long before Curt ever fell through the ice and into the freezing water. This was a harmless situation, but the more important and obvious question is, "Can we see when we've ventured onto thin ice in our everyday lives?" The story of Samson gives us a perspective on living a strong Christian life that keeps us away from such a plunge.

The Old Testament book of Judges tells the story of Samson, a man who becomes the leader of his nation. Samson's birth is foretold by an angel (Judges 13:3), and his destiny is to deliver Israel out of the hands of the Philistines. Samson is a Nazarite, meaning he has separated himself for special service to God, and by virtue of his vow he cannot drink wine, cut his hair or beard, or touch a dead body or eat unclean (prohibited) foods.

Samson has a strong starting point. He has a clear mission, and he has taken steps to serve God and no one else. But as Samson's life progresses, he begins to walk toward thin ice, and the closer he gets to the edge, the less God can use him. The root of Samson's problem is that he becomes more concerned with his personal needs than his mission to serve God and others.

We may know Samson for the tremendous physical strength he demonstrates on many occasions. For example, he kills a lion with his bare hands (Judges 14:5-6) and even slays a thousand Philistines using the jawbone of a donkey as his weapon. On another occasion, when surrounded by his enemies inside a walled city, he simply goes to the city's main gate, uproots the large doors and the posts that hold them, and carries them to the top of a nearby hill (Judges 16:3). Samson's amazing physical strength seems to increase throughout his life, but soon his spiritual power is on the decrease.

Samson decides to marry a woman who fails to meet the approval of his parents. She does not share their faith and values, and she turns out to be untrustworthy as well. But we are told in Judges 14:4 that this is for a reason: "His parents did not know that this was from the LORD, who was seeking an occasion to confront the Philistines; for at that time they were ruling over Israel."

For the next two chapters, Samson whips the Philistines with a mighty show of strength. He even ties the tails of foxes together, places hot firebrands on their tails, and turns them loose on the countryside to burn the Philistine's crops.

Is Samson justified in doing all this? There is disagreement over this point. At least in the beginning, we are told that the Lord is behind these actions and is using them to bring judgment against the Philistines. But by the time we get to Judges 16, Samson is clearly doing things that are contrary to God's plan. I lean toward the view that Samson is losing focus on what he is supposed to do, which is to "begin the deliverance of Israel from the hands of the Philistines" (Judges 13:5). Here's why:

Samson's love for God begins to be divided. He goes to Gaza and finds a prostitute with whom he spends time. He follows this up with a relationship with the infamous Delilah, who is not someone he should be spending time with if he is intent on serving God. Delilah doesn't share his beliefs and goals and is intent on destroying him.

Delilah desires to know the source of Samson's strength so that her countrymen can at last subdue him. It is clear she wants to destroy Samson, but he desires her so much that he is perfectly willing to go back to her house day after day. He lies about the source of his strength and then watches as Delilah calls upon her Philistines to capture him, knowing that his strength is still with him.

Samson's life reminds me of the electric fences we use to keep cattle in their pastures. The electric fence wire is about three feet above the ground, but as the summer grass grows taller and taller, it eventually touches the wire. The fence still has "shock value," but the more grass that grows up the fence, the more electricity is siphoned off the line.

We have a tester we clamp onto the wire to see exactly how much electricity is flowing, and sometimes we have to cut the grass from under the fence to get that reading back to where it should be. If we don't, the fence eventually has no value at all and the cattle simply walk over the top of it.

Samson's life, like that fence, is nearly overgrown. He needs one of those fence testers to see that the strength he has to serve God is slowly weakening as his life becomes consumed with the wrong things. He needs to take steps to cut out all the bad things in his life. Instead, he tells Delilah the truth…his strength is found in his long hair. Here's something very important to remember: Samson's strength is not actually contained in his hair: it is the Spirit of God that gives him his strength. Remember, Samson's uncut hair is a symbol of his Nazarite vow, a vow that demonstrates his life is devoted to service to God.

After she learns his secret, Delilah has a man cut Samson's hair while he sleeps, and now his strength, both symbolically and literally, is taken from him. Judges 16:20-21 tells us, "Then she called, 'Samson, the Philistines are upon you!'

"He awoke from his sleep and thought, 'I'll go out as before and shake myself free.' But he did not know that the LORD had left him.

"Then the Philistines seized him, gouged out his eyes and took him down to Gaza. Binding him with bronze shackles, they set him to grinding in the prison."

Splash! Samson has just fallen through the ice.

Notice the phrase, "I'll go out as before and shake myself free." That's how sin works. We become numb to the effect it has upon us. Samson doesn't realize that the power he has to serve God is slowly draining away as he spends more and more time with Delilah. This begins even before he meets her because he puts himself in provocative situations. He allows his emotions to pull him away from his mission to serve God. We have to be aware of this in our own lives, too.

The Philistines begin to party. They've just defeated their nemesis, a man whose physical strength is no match for any of them, and they are bent on humiliating and mocking him. In fact, they even hold a celebration in honor of their gods who they believe helped them conquer this mighty man of Israel. Samson is brought before the crowd and chained to two pillars.

Fortunately, he has had some time to think about his life. He has reflected on his failures and how he has shut God out of his life, even though God never stopped loving him and desiring to use him to do his work.

As we walk further from God and closer to thin ice, the ways God can use us become limited. At this point in his life, Samson has to get out of the water and walk back toward God to be of use again. Sometimes we have to stop and walk back toward the safe side of the pool, too.

We are told that Samson's hair begins to grow again, and I believe this is a symbol that Samson has reconciled himself with God. The sign of his Nazarite vow is now apparent again, and Samson's desire to serve God is rekindled.

As Samson stands chained between the pillars at the banquet, he asks God for strength one last time, knowing that he will die in his effort to slay his captors. Samson pushes down the pillars to which he is chained, and those pillars that support the building let the roof topple in upon him and those gathered there. The Bible says that Samson slays more people in this final act than he has in all his life previously.

I believe God gives us strength just like he did Samson. We may not have brute physical strength, but each of us has abilities that can be used to serve God. What obstacles keep us from using those abilities to their fullest? What actions do we take that move us further from God and closer to precariously thin ice?

There comes a point in Samson's life when he is so far from God that his life cannot be used to serve him as it once had. Like Samson, we can ask forgiveness, repent, and once again become close to God, but God doesn't want us to move to the thin side of the reflecting pool in the first place. On that side, there isn't much room to maneuver and our range is limited. God wants us to walk back to Him and to experience a powerful life of service. If we live for God, like Samson, he will use us to do mighty things for Him.

CHAPTER 6

Who Are You?

MILWAUKEE, WISCONSIN

"I tell you the truth," Jesus answered,
"before Abraham was born, I am!"

—JOHN 8:58

It's a restaurant with almost no advertising. In fact, the owners want you to have to ask directions to find it. It sounds odd, but that's the point. It's called the Safe House, a restaurant and pub in downtown Milwaukee. There are no flashing neon signs or billboards to direct your way. Just as in a spy movie, this is a "safe house," a secret place that requires a secret code to enter.

Even upon entering the side door, which is entered via an alley, you might think you have the wrong place. A telephone operator, seated in front of a 1950's-style switchboard, greets you. But once you tell her the password (or get the password from her, which usually requires that you perform a dance that is secretly shown to all those already inside the restaurant), a wall behind you swivels open to reveal a secret tunnel.

The idea of a secret password reflects the importance we sometimes place on names. Think of the entertainers Marilyn Monroe, Madonna, Mark Twain, Sting, Shania Twain, and Muhammad Ali. None of these is the entertainers' real names. At least, they are not the names these individuals were given at birth. Even in the radio and TV business, I know people who have changed their names for a variety of reasons.

But who is God? What about God's name? Where does God come from? What does he do? These are tough questions, but it's not as if God doesn't give us some of the answers. God says plenty about himself. He speaks of who he is and how he wants us to live, and a lot of these insights are found in his very name. Let's make three stops in the Bible to three places that might seem totally unrelated, but that reveal something very special about God.

You might remember the story of Moses and the burning bush. It's found in Exodus 3. Moses is tending to his father-in-law's sheep when he sees a bush on fire, but the fire does not burn up the bush. When Moses comes closer, the bush speaks to him! It is God in the form of fire. God tells Moses that he will be the man to return to Egypt and lead the Hebrew people out of slavery. One of Moses' objections to this is, "Who should I tell them sent me?"

It's a logical question. If Moses shows up and says, "I'm leading you all out of here!" the people are probably going to say, "Who are you and who sent you?" Just as if I showed up at the Safe House in Milwaukee the telephone operator would want to know the password to let me in, Moses asks God a question we might ask ourselves: "Who are you?"

God answers by telling Moses that his name is "I AM" (Exodus 3:14).

That seems like a strange name. I don't know anyone with a name like that. Once I was speaking to a group of junior high students and one young man asked me, "Does that mean that God's first name is 'I' and his last name is 'AM'?"

I guess I hadn't thought of it that way. The name "I AM" is so much different than anything else we have ever heard that we don't know how to interpret it. In most Bibles, the letters are all capitalized, giving it extra importance. So what does God mean when he says his name is "I AM"?

I don't watch much pro wrestling, but in preparing for this chapter, I took a break from my work and flipped through the TV channels. As I quickly scanned the line-up, a wrestler caught my eye, a wrestler wearing a shirt with a very interesting sentence on the back. The shirt stated, "The BEST…IS, WAS, EVER WILL BE." Sounds catchy. However, I don't think the wrestler thought a lot about what his T-shirt was saying.

Think about it. If he holds the title belt right now, then he can say that he "IS" the best. However, he says he not only "IS" the best, he also "WAS" the best and "WILL BE" the best in the future. At this point we have a problem.

This wrestler must never have been born and must never die in order to say this. If there were people living before he was born and I think we can safely assume there were, someone else "WAS" the best, because he wasn't even around to wrestle. If the wrestler says he "EVER WILL BE" the best, he must not plan on dying. If he dies, then he will no longer be here to defend his title. That means someone else "WILL BE" the best.

So unless this wrestler was born before anyone else and plans on out-living everyone, he is going to have a tough time defending the statement on his shirt. In fact, there is only one person who can rightfully wear that T-shirt: God. That's the title God uses for himself when Moses asks him his name at the burning bush. The only difference is, God shortens it to only two words: "I AM."

If God says his name is "I AM," that means he has ALWAYS been present. "I AM" literally means "the self-existent one." Only someone who has ALWAYS been present in the world, or self-existent, can say they are the eternal "I AM." Think about that. God is always in the present tense. God IS always here.

Let's fast-forward to our second stop, the book of Matthew and the birth of Jesus. We are told that Jesus is born in a manger in the town of Bethlehem, and soon after wise men from the east come to Herod, asking, "Where is he that is born king of the Jews?" Just imagine how this goes over with King Herod!

Several wise men arrive. There could well have been far more than three wise men who traveled to see Herod, but because three gifts are presented to the baby Jesus, we usually assume there were three wise men. I often jokingly tell audiences to remember that these were *men*. We guys are notorious for pooling our money and getting one gift on behalf of several of us so we don't all have to go shopping! But seriously, the Bible says Herod and the entire city of Jerusalem were "troubled" (Matthew 2:3). Would a mere three men from the east "trouble" a king and a large city? No one knows for sure.

Those wise men basically ask the king, "King Herod, where is the new king who was just born? We've seen his star in the skies."

The wise men state that they've seen a star that foretells the birth of the king. Not only is it amazing that a star guides them, it is amazing that they know to look for it. Remember, these wise men live in the east, far from the Jews, yet they know the scriptures. In Numbers 24:17, a prophecy proclaims, "I see him, but not now; I behold him, but not near. A star will come out of Jacob; a scepter will rise out of Israel." They know these words, and when they see the star, they know what it means.

Herod is a cruel, yet sly, king. As king, he is not about to let anyone take the throne from him. However, for him to say to the wise men, "Where is he? I've got to go kill him!" would incite even more trouble. So Herod tells them to find the child so that he might "worship him also" (Matthew 2:8).

The wise men do find the baby, though by the time they arrive, Jesus might well be a whole year older due to the time they've spent traveling. When they see him, something amazing happens...they fall down and worship him! There are others in the room, yet the wise men bow before the baby!

Today we recognize this event on January 6, a date known as the Epiphany, a word that means "reveal." These were not Jewish men, but gentiles, who by their worship of the child Jesus "reveal" to the world that he will be a savior to all mankind.

The wise men don't return to King Herod because they have been warned in a dream not to do so. They know that Herod has evil intentions. Once Herod sees that the wise men aren't going to return, he sends soldiers to Bethlehem to kill all the children younger than two years of age. Jesus and his mother and father escape to Egypt to avoid the slaughter.

Let's fast-forward one final time, to John 8. Jesus has now grown into his early thirties and is discussing the scriptures with the Jews. At one point in their dialogue they plainly ask, "Who are you?" It is the question that causes Moses to turn aside and examine the burning bush. It is the question that causes wise men to travel from the east and Herod to kill all the babies in Bethlehem. It is the question that people still ask today. "Who is this Jesus?"

As Jesus continues his discussion with the Jews, he says he was present when Abraham lived. The Jews can't believe it! Here is a man in his early thirties saying he was present when Abraham lived. He would have to be thousands of years old for that to be true. But in John 8:58, Jesus makes a statement that goes far beyond what he has just said: "Before Abraham was born, I am." Jesus uses the exact same title that God uses when speaking to Moses from the burning bush. Mathematically, the equation looks like this: Exodus 3:14 = John 8:58.

The Jews know exactly what Jesus is claiming: Jesus is claiming he is God. He is the God who speaks to Moses from the burning bush.

He is the baby whom wise men recognize as their savior. He is the man who stands before them and uses a phrase that no one else but God can claim. By using the term "I AM," he is stating that he has always existed, from eternity in the past to eternity in the future. That's why they pick up stones to kill him. Make no mistake; they know this isn't some joke Jesus is trying to make. He is claiming to be God.

C. S. Lewis comes right to the point in his book *Mere Christianity*: "You can shut Him up for a fool, you can spit at Him and kill Him as a demon; or you can fall at His feet and call Him Lord and God. But let us not come with any patronizing nonsense about His being a great human teacher. He has not left that open to us. He did not intend to."

Jesus isn't like some music stars or radio personalities. He gives us his real name. The following question perhaps should be turned toward each of us: who are you? Do we believe Jesus' claim to be God? Do we believe he is our Savior? If we do believe that, do we honor and give Him reverence as Moses and the wise men did? Do we live our lives knowing we have a God who is in control, a God who has existed and will exist for all time?

Who are you?

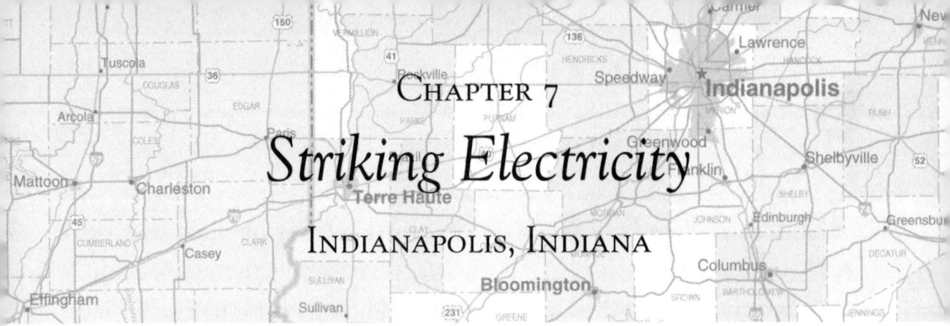

CHAPTER 7

Striking Electricity

INDIANAPOLIS, INDIANA

And I will ask the Father, and he will give you another Counselor to be with you forever—the Spirit of truth. The world cannot accept him, because it neither sees him nor knows him. But you know him, for he lives with you and will be in you.

—JOHN 14:16-17

Growing up on a farm, you never know what a day will bring. Because there's always so much to do, we often split up to cover more ground. One day my father sent my granddad and me to work on a fence that needed repair. The fence wasn't very tall and it only covered a small area, but though it had iron bars, it needed more support. We decided to drive a couple of new posts in between the old ones to make the entire fence more sturdy (and to keep the cattle on the right side of the fence).

This wasn't supposed to be a big job. All I had to do was drive two posts into the ground and tie the bars of the fence to them. As I began to drive the steel fence posts into the ground with a large sledgehammer, my muscles quickly began to tire. The ground was hard, since it had not rained for many days, and the posts had to be driven about three feet into the ground. It was tough work.

I finally made it to the second post, but now I swung the hammer over and over with little result. Granddad could tell I was tired. He couldn't help since he was too old to swing the big hammer, but he decided to cheer me on.

"Hit it harder!" he exclaimed above the ping of the hammer hitting the steel. He laughed and yelled more encouragement and clapped in approval as I picked up the pace and slowly began to drive the post into the earth.

Soon I was hitting the steel post so hard that sparks began to fly with the friction of steel on steel. I swung the hammer harder, inspired by the sparks I was generating from my punishing blows. I could tell Granddad was pleased too. We were making real progress now!

Then I made an important discovery...the steel post was generating sparks even when I wasn't hitting it. Yes...I had driven the post directly into an underground electric line! Talk about your electric fence!

I could make a horrible pun at this point like, "We were shocked!" However, "We were lucky!" is more like it. I had come into contact with a tremendous power, and that power was making its presence known. It's a power much like the one that can reside in you.

When Christ ascended into heaven, he said he would not leave us comfortless. He would send someone for us. That person is the Holy Spirit. John 14:15-26 records the passage in which Jesus describes the coming of the Holy Spirit: "And I will ask the Father, and he will give you another Counselor to be with you forever—the Spirit of truth. The world cannot accept him, because it neither sees him nor knows him. But you know him, for he lives with you and will be in you."

The Holy Spirit is sometimes difficult to describe, but the Spirit is a lot like the electricity I had come into contact with as I drove the steel posts. I can look at an electric line and guess there is probably a lot of electricity running through it. I can know there is electricity running through it if I touch it (or drive a steel post into it). I can see the product of that electricity when I turn on the lights or use an appliance.

A believer in Christ is much the same. When we answer the call of the Spirit and make a commitment to follow Christ as our Savior, the Bible says that Christ comes to dwell in us in the form of the Holy Spirit. John 14:17 and Galatians 4:6 reveal that the Holy Spirit resides inside believers when they accept Christ into their hearts in faith. But just like the electricity we can't see, understanding the Holy Spirit is sometimes difficult.

In Indianapolis you can visit the home of President Benjamin Harrison. He was elected to the White House in 1888 and served just one term. It was while Harrison was president that his wife, Caroline, obtained an appropriation from Congress that allowed for refurbishing the executive mansion. One of the improvements the Harrisons made was the addition of electricity. One would think that the president of the United States would immediately embrace the use of the new power source throughout the White House, but the Harrisons may have been scared of the new convenience. This might explain why the gentleman who installed the light switches in the White House was retained to turn them on and off. He remained employed at the White House for forty-two years, although he eventually graduated from "light switch duty."

Just imagine a job description that includes turning on and off light switches because the owners of the house are scared to do so! There are reports that the Harrisons were so concerned about an electric shock from the circuit that they once left the lights on all night rather than touch the switches.

The Harrisons had electric power when few other Americans did, yet they were afraid of it. They might never have gotten any use from it at all had it not been for employees who assisted them.

My home has electric lines that run to it, and I have a virtually unlimited supply of electricity. Unless I try to turn on something equivalent to the lights at Times Square on New Year's Eve, I will get all the electricity I want (provided I pay my bill). But the issue is still similar to the Harrison's...do I use that power?

From God's perspective, do I use the power available to me? The issue is not whether we get more of the Holy Spirit; it is instead whether the Holy Spirit gets more of us. We must live our lives in ways that allow the Spirit to work in and through us. Think of it this way: in John 14:23, Jesus says the Spirit will make his "home" or abode inside of us.

What can we do to make the Spirit feel at home? Important things like obeying God's word, praying, sharing our faith with others, and showing kindness to others make the Holy Spirit feel at home.

When we obey God's word, we tap into a surprising current of unlimited power. Galatians 5:22-23 describes the fruit of the Spirit as love, joy, peace, long-suffering (courage and endurance), gentleness (kindness), goodness, faith, meekness (power under control), and self-control. These are nine fruits we can each taste more of if we let the Spirit have more of us.

We can know the Spirit is working in us by the fruit our lives produce, just as we know there is electricity in our electric lines by the appliances we see running in our homes. Our appliances are turned on. Are we?

Chapter 8

Looking Inside

Salt Lake City, Utah

The LORD does not look at the things man looks at. Man looks at the outward appearance, but the LORD looks at the heart.

—I Samuel 16:7

The man was intriguing. Put him in the middle of farm country and he might blend in a little bit, but in the departure lounge of a flight bound for Salt Lake City, he conspicuously stood out. People tried not to stare, but you could tell the same question was on everybody's mind: "Why and where was this man flying?"

He wore the traditional black broad-rimmed hat, black coat, and suspenders of an old order Amish farmer and looked to be in his mid-70s. I thought we might have acquaintances in common, since I have Amish friends who do blacksmith work for us. Although the Amish do travel, sometimes taking long trips across the country to see relatives, it certainly was rare to see such a gentlemen in an airport. I wondered if perhaps he was flying to meet some of his family, or perhaps there was another reason. It wasn't any of my business, but I was curious.

As I settled into my seat, this very man stopped at my aisle and took the seat next to me. We exchanged hellos, after which I opened up the conversation with, "So where are you headed today? Are you stopping in Salt Lake or heading somewhere else?" I didn't figure I was being too nosy; most travelers exchange such information.

He smiled and with a soft voice said, "Well, I've got a big trip ahead of me."

"Oh really?" I countered with a raised eyebrow. "Ya headed to the west coast?"

"No, a little farther than that...I'm headed to China."

China? Was he pulling my leg? Why in the world would this man be headed to China? Was it the vacation he'd always dreamed of? "Wow, that's a long trip," I responded. "Is that a place you've always dreamed of visiting?"

"Oh, this is my eighth trip," he stated with a grin. "I'm going for business."

I consider myself a well-worn traveler, but eight trips to China? What on earth could be the reason an Amish gentlemen would need to visit China so frequently? Was he an entrepreneur using the Amish as a guise to get the inside track on a big deal?

"You see, in my community we don't use electricity," he explained, unsure of whether I knew much about the Amish way of life. "I run a store in our community that sells oil lamps, but no one in this country makes them anymore. That's why I go to China...to visit the factories that make them and then place an order for what we will need for the next two or three years."

As we continued our conversation, I reflected on how much my perception of the situation was changing. It is human nature to look at the outward situation and make a judgment on what is before us. I'd figured this Amish man was probably making his first flight when in reality he had already traveled seven times to a nation most people never see.

The Bible speaks much of appearances. In fact, in the book of First Samuel, the prophet Samuel is told by God to anoint the next king of Israel. The current king, Saul, has turned away from God and

Samuel is directed to go to the house of Jesse in Bethlehem where he will find the new king.

When he arrives at Jesse's house, Samuel immediately sees who the next king of the country will be. Eliab, the oldest son, is clearly the man for the job. He's not only the eldest, but he's tall and strong and has the look of a king.

We often have a "look" we associate with certain professions. What does a fireman look like? How about a farmer? Or even the president of the United States? During presidential election years, you often hear people say that a certain candidate seems more "presidential." This man, Eliab, looks "kingly." Surely he's the man Samuel is supposed to choose.

We don't know for sure how God speaks to Samuel, but the message is clear. He says to Samuel, "Do not consider his appearance or his height…The LORD does not look at the things man looks at. Man looks at the outward appearance, but the LORD looks at the heart" (1 Samuel 16:7).

Those are beautiful words! God looks at the heart! Thank goodness he does, because regardless of how we look on the outside, God wants to be the ruler of our hearts.

Samuel asks Jesse to have the next eldest son pass before him, then the next, and so on, until this scene is repeated seven times. Each time God essentially says, "This isn't the one." What is Samuel supposed to do now? Jesse is out of sons. Can't one of the seven measure up?

Samuel asks Jesse if that is all of his sons and Jesse tells him, "Well, I've got one more son. He's the youngest and he's out in the countryside watching over the sheep." The son is just a teenager, but it is David God has chosen. So, at God's command, Samuel anoints David as the next king of Israel in Bethlehem. It is over a thousand years before another king is anointed in the same city, when Jesus is anointed king by the wise men who travel from the east.

At this point, the story already speaks volumes. How many times does outward appearance influence us to keep our distance from someone? Young or old, black or white, rich or poor, a multitude of appearances influences the way we act.

One of the best moments I have ever experienced in a church was on the south side of Chicago at Salem Baptist Church. A friend of mine, Corey, attends services there, and he invited me to join him one weekend when I was in town.

Before we go further, there is something I should tell you about outward appearances…I am a white guy from rural Missouri. My friend Corey is a black guy from Chicago, and Salem Baptist's parishioners are predominately black.

What a service! I have never experienced singing like that anywhere else in the country. I stood up, clapped, swayed, and sang my heart out. Corey was up in the choir, but despite the difference in my outward appearance, I seemed to melt into the crowd.

What touched me was the conclusion of the service, when Pastor Meeks asked if anyone would like to join Salem Baptist. He invited those individuals to come down front and soon several people were making their way toward him. At this point a nice gentlemen who had sat next to me the entire service reached over and tapped me on the knee. He smiled and whispered, "If you'd like to go down, I'll walk with you so you don't have to go alone."

I've often reflected on what that man did. Based on outward appearances, I probably didn't seem to fit in. Because the color of my skin was different, I was most likely a visitor. This man could see that Corey had brought me to church. Why should he bother inviting me to go down front when my friend would be a much more logical choice to do that? There were many reasons why this man should never have given a single thought to me, but he did give me a thought! He valued me for what was inside me, just as God does. Not only that, he offered to "walk with me", so that I might feel more at home.

How would we have responded if we had been in that man's shoes? We encounter such situations all the time, yet the scene on the outside influences our decisions. God calls us to see those around us in a different way. He wants us to look at the heart.

Not only does God want us to value the "inside" of others, he wants us to take a good long look at our own hearts. Isn't it interesting that David, the man God chooses by looking at his heart, would write in Psalms 139:23 and 24, "Search me, O God, and know my heart; test me and know my anxious thoughts. See if there is any offensive way in me, and lead me in the way everlasting."

David wants God to show him his own flaws so he can correct them. It is only by having a clean heart that David can fully serve God. But looking at our own hearts is a difficult thing. Sometimes we're too close to the situation to see our own sin.

Back in fourth grade, I remember trying out for something called Kinder Khorus. This was a singing group composed of fourth, fifth, and sixth graders that traveled to area schools and put on performances. I really wanted to be in the group, but you had to go through try-outs and be selected. For your audition you could either sing a solo or a duet in front of the music teacher. I wasn't about to sing a solo, but one of my classmates and I picked out a song we could sing together.

I suppose we did all right. It's kind of hard to judge your singing ability when you are a fourth grader, but I anxiously awaited the day when the results would be posted. The list was to go up outside the music room door on Friday morning, but on Thursday afternoon I heard a rumor the list had been posted early. Yes, there it was…the list! I ran over to the door to scroll through the fourth graders' names. There was Doug…but no Andrew.

Doug made it but not me? That didn't make any sense. I was at least as good as he was. Besides, we'd sung a duet. How could the teacher pick one of us and not the other? I'd heard him sing. "I'm a lot better than he is" is what my critical fourth grade mind thought.

I was crushed. I went home and cried. I told mother that Kinder Khorus was ruined. With Doug involved, those performances were certainly not going to be very good. The music teacher had picked all the wrong kids.

"You're sure you're not just a little jealous of Doug, are you? Maybe he's better than you think," whispered Mother.

"He's awful. He can't carry a tune at all. The teacher must have heard me and thought it was him," I complained.

I went to school the next morning dreading the sight of Doug, who I was sure would be touting his selection. In music class that morning, the teacher had a surprise for me.

"I hear that some of you saw a list outside my door yesterday," she stated. "Well, there was a mistake. The secretary didn't get all the names I asked her to type. You probably wondered why our group had shrunk by ten students this year. I've put the new list up and you can all take turns looking at it before we begin class."

"There's still a shot," I said to myself. I scanned the list quickly, looking for my spot in alphabetical order. There it was! I'd made it! Doug was on the list, too. That was nice. He was, after all, my friend.

When I got home, I ran to tell Mother the great news. She listened intently as I shared the story. For some reason, she didn't seem to smile as much as I'd thought she would.

She shook her head and said, "That's nice…but it sure is too bad that Doug is still a part of the group. His voice will ruin it for you, won't it?"

Funny how we see things from a different angle all of sudden. Doug was great all along; it was my jealously that led me to say what I had about him. It was as plain as day. Mom had turned the spotlight right back around on my heart, and I didn't like what I saw.

If you read about the life of David in the Bible, you will see that he had some similar experiences to mine, only the stakes were much higher than making it in an elementary school singing group. His lust for a woman got him into big trouble. He had a friend, Nathan, who got him on track and showed him his faults (II Samuel 11 and 12). Of course, we want to head off such problems before they begin. In either case, good friends who hold us accountable for our actions can be a very important part of our lives.

God looks at our hearts, and no matter what we've done in the past, he can use us for the future if we are willing to make our insides right before him. Think about it. God uses Paul, who is an accessory to murder; Rahab, a prostitute; Mark, a coward who runs from responsibility but later becomes courageous for Christ and writes one of the gospels; and Moses, a man who leads his people out of Egypt yet is a self-proclaimed poor speaker. God wants to use each one of us.

God not only calls us to take a new look at others, he also calls us to look inside ourselves. He wants us to examine the evil and sin we harbor in our own lives. Sometimes that's tough to see. We're blinded by it because we've lived with some of it for so long, but others can see it and help us remove it and stay away from it in the future.

Finally, God wants to use each of us in a special way to serve him. He can do that only when our insides are set on Him.

Chapter 9

Game Plan for Defeating a Christian

Green Bay, Wisconsin

Be strong and courageous. Do not be afraid or discouraged because of the king of Assyria and the vast army with him, for there is a greater power with us than with him. With him is only the arm of flesh, but with us is the LORD our God to help us and to fight our battles.

—2 Chronicles 32:7-8

On Christmas Day when I was seven years old, my father gave me a gift that I still cherish today. He gave me his Lionel train set, complete with a locomotive, several rail cars, and many buildings I could use for landscaping. Because of its age, the train set was already worth a lot, but it's worth even more to me in terms of the fun I've had with it and its sentimental value.

I've always enjoyed trains, so when I headed to Green Bay, Wisconsin, to do a story at the National Railroad Museum, I was really looking forward to it. There are many outstanding old locomotives and other rail stock there, but one of the most impressive displays is a locomotive and two rail cars used during the 1940s. Known as the Eisenhower Collection, this locomotive and two coaches were used by the general and other military staff during World War II.

Officially the "London & North Eastern No. 1591 and 1592," these coaches were the home of much of the planning for the D-Day invasion at Normandy. No. 1592 was codenamed "Bayonet" and was used extensively in 1944 by Eisenhower to tour bases and visit commanders as they prepared for the massive assault. For security reasons, most trips took place at night, and the windows of the steel-sided car were often covered in compliance with blackout rules.

The exhibit is amazing, especially when one considers the magnitude of the battle plans that were made inside those coaches. A "plan" is a very important part of winning a war, and a lot of time is taken to make sure that plan doesn't fall into the wrong hands.

The Old Testament tells the story of a very interesting war plan. Not only does it speak of how to wage a battle, it also tells how one army worked to demoralize the nation they were seeking to defeat. It is a battle plan for destroying a nation faithful to God.

One of the leaders in that ancient battle was a king named Hezekiah. He was only twenty-five when he became king, and he reigned over the kingdom of Judah for twenty-nine years. (At this time in history, Israel had split into two kingdoms, the northern kingdom called "Israel" and the southern kingdom called "Judah.")

The Bible says, "Hezekiah trusted in the LORD, the God of Israel. There was no one like him among all the kings of Judah, either before him or after him. He held fast to the LORD and did not cease to follow him; he kept the commands the LORD had given Moses. And the LORD was with him; he was successful in whatever he undertook" (2 Kings 18:5-7).

In the fourteenth year of Hezekiah's reign, he meets a formidable foe, the Assyrians, under the leadership of Sennacherib. In the Old Testament, we read about the planning that takes place for that war. 2 Kings 18 and 19, 2 Chronicles 31 and 32, and Isaiah 36 and 37 all provide information about the confrontation.

Sennacherib sends his top military officials as well as a great number of troops toward Jerusalem. Once there, they tell the people just how foolish it is for Hezekiah to believe that God will save them. 2 Kings 18:19-20 records these words: "The field commander said to them, 'Tell Hezekiah: This is what the great king, the king of Assyria, says: On what are you basing this confidence of yours? You say you have strategy and military strength—but you speak only empty words.'"

Their strategy is to take the city without a fight. If they can persuade the people of Jerusalem that Hezekiah is leading them to certain death, they might revolt against him and choose to join the Assyrians.

Sennacherbib's leaders keep up their verbal assault. "This is what the king says: Do not let Hezekiah deceive you. He cannot deliver you from my hand. Do not let Hezekiah persuade you to trust in the LORD when he says, 'The LORD will surely deliver us; this city will not be given into the hand of the king of Assyria.' Do not listen to Hezekiah. This is what the king of Assyria says: Make peace with me and come out to me. Then every one of you will eat from his own vine and fig tree and drink water from his own cistern, until I come and take you to a land like your own, a land of grain and new wine, a land of bread and vineyards, a land of olive trees and honey. Choose life and not death!" (II King 18:29-32).

In Chapter 4, I discuss how Satan tries to deceive us and make us believe he offers us something that God cannot. This exactly mirrors what the Assyrians say to the inhabitants of Jerusalem: "Why follow God and die? Join us and live. If you join us, you can live in a land just as nice as what you have now." It is the Assyrians' game plan to defeat the followers of God.

Armies have waged wars of words for centuries. Before the D-Day invasion, General Eisenhower recorded the following message that was played for the soldiers who would soon be facing their enemy: "You are about to embark upon the Great Crusade, toward which we have striven these many months. The eyes of the world are upon you. The hopes and prayers of liberty-loving people everywhere march with you. In company with our brave Allies and brothers-in-arms on other fronts, you will bring about the destruction of the German war machine, the elimination of Nazi tyranny over the oppressed peoples of Europe, and security for ourselves in a free world. Your task will not be an easy one. Your enemy is well trained, well equipped, and battle-hardened. He will fight savagely."

Hezekiah spoke to his people before the battle with the Assyrians and reminded them of God's power: "Be strong and courageous. Do not be afraid or discouraged because of the king of Assyria and the vast army with him, for there is a greater power with us than with him. With him is only the arm of flesh, but with us is the LORD our God to help us and to fight our battles" (2 Chronicles 32:7-8).

Centuries later, Eisenhower concluded his inspirational words to his troops by reminding them of God's power to overcome their foe. "I have full confidence in your courage, devotion to duty, and skill in battle. We will accept nothing less than full victory! Good luck! And let us all beseech the blessing of Almighty God upon this great and noble undertaking."

There is no battle between the Assyrians and Jerusalem. God takes care of the army and puts an end to the man who taunted God's people. 2 Kings 19:35-37 records, "That night the angel of the LORD went out and put to death a hundred and eighty-five thousand men in the Assyrian camp. When the people got up the next morning—there were all the dead bodies! So Sennacherib king of Assyria broke camp and withdrew. He returned to Nineveh and stayed there. One day, while he was worshiping in the temple of his god Nisroch, his sons Adrammelech and Sharezer cut him down with the sword, and they escaped to the land of Ararat. And Esarhaddon his son succeeded him as king."

The game plan to defeat a Christian has always been to cast doubt about God and offer a "better" way. It is what Sennacherib did, and what many others since him have done. Over and over Christians are called to doubt that God exists or that he will make good on his promises. Yet, as the Assyrians learned, God won't abandon his people. We would do well to remember Hezekiah's words to the citizens of Jerusalem: "There is a greater power with us than with him. With him is only the arm of flesh, but with us is the LORD our God to help us and to fight our battles."

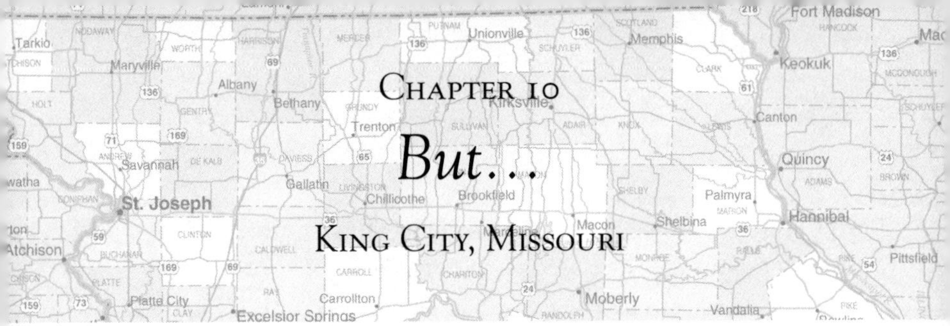

Chapter 10

But...

King City, Missouri

Then Caleb silenced the people before Moses and said, "We should go up and take possession of the land, for we can certainly do it."

Numbers 13:30

When I played football in junior high, our locker room was underneath the elementary school building. I suppose that makes it a basement, but it was really more like a dungeon. The place was damp, the paint on the old concrete walls was half peeled, and a putrid smell often wafted through the place. To top it off, toads inhabited its dark corners, sometimes making themselves known as they moved from one side to the other.

Whether it was for a practice or a game, that's where we dressed. On this night, we were ready to hit the field for a football contest against a neighboring school. To get to the field, we ascended a long, narrow set of steps that took us out of the dungeon. (It is still called the "dungeon" today. It is no longer used as a locker room, but rather as the school's tornado shelter, adding extra terror to an already scary situation.) Once on ground level, we walked down an alley between the school buildings that led to the field.

On this night, as we ascended the stairs and stepped into the alley, we noticed that the opponent's bus was already parked in the lane just ahead of us. In fact, the other team had come dressed and was now standing around the bus looking at the field. They hadn't even noticed our team standing about fifty yards behind them, waiting for our coach to lead us onto the field.

It doesn't seem like much of a story, except that our high school's junior varsity team was still practicing on the field. For some reason they were wearing their game jerseys as they finished up the last few minutes of their scrimmage before we took to the field for our game. As the opposing team now stared at the field, they supposed they were seeing the team they were about to play.

There were only a couple of year's difference in age between our team and that JV team, but those couple of years meant that each of those players looked like a giant compared to the stature of we mere junior highers. With the opponents now looking at the JV team, we could hear them talk about how big each of our players was.

"Look at number 77," we heard them say. "He's got to be six feet tall!"

Another countered, "I thought coach said they've only won one game. He was lying."

For those brief moments, our little junior high team saw fear sweep across the neighboring school that supposed they had run into a team that might as well have been from the NFL.

I suppose I can't fault the other school for believing they were about to be pummeled as they looked at our JV on the field, but what if the differences in size didn't really matter? What if they were one hundred percent sure that no matter how big or how experienced the other team was, they would win?

My line of questioning may sound a little absurd, but you and I often have trouble getting the right perspective on the challenges that lie in front of us in real life, let alone a football game.

It's a situation that literally plays out in the wilderness east of Egypt. The nation of Israel serves as slaves to the people of Egypt until Moses leads them out of bondage, finally freeing them in their miraculous crossing of the Red Sea. God has promised the children of Israel the land of Canaan, a fruitful land where they can live and raise bountiful crops. Deuteronomy 1:20-21 says, "You have reached the hill country of the Amorites, which the LORD our God is giving us. See, the LORD your God has given you the land. Go up and take possession of it as the LORD, the God of your fathers, told you. Do not be afraid; do not be discouraged."

Unfortunately, before this mighty nation of people enters Canaan, they are afflicted with the same disease many of us get today...a case of the "Buts." They begin to see all the reasons why they can't achieve what God has already promised them, and they fail to live their lives with the knowledge of these promises.

God has promised us much. He has promised eternal life in heaven for those who believe in Him as their Savior (John 3:16-18, Romans 10:9). He promises that the Holy Spirit will never leave his believers and that all things work for the ultimate good of God's children (Romans 8:26-28). God promises that his love will never cease, even at times when we may feel far from Him (Romans 8:35-39). God also promises to forgive us our sins when we confess them to him (I John 1:9).

These are just some of the many promises God makes to us, but when we lose sight of these promises, we begin to alter our lives in ways we should not.

As God's people leave Egypt behind and see the promised land before them, they send spies to scout the area to observe the bounty and size up the enemy. This seems logical, although God has already promised them the land. Their actions here are beginning to reflect disbelief rather than belief in what God can and will do for them.

I remember one time when I was playing little league baseball and my coach told me to steal second on the next pitch. I was standing on first base, so I took my lead and watched the pitcher go into his wind-up and deliver the ball to home plate. For some reason

I froze and didn't run. I didn't think I could make it, and I was afraid I would be thrown out at second base.

My coach, standing only three feet from me, lashed out, "Why didn't you run? Why are you still here? They aren't going to throw to second base; there's a runner on third."

What the coach was referring to was the fact that at this level of play, teams never tried to throw out a runner stealing second when another runner was already on third base. If they threw the ball to second base, the runner from third would come home to score. Though I was still safe at first, I was not at second base where I should be by now, and if the next batter got a hit, it would be more difficult for me to score. The issue was not whether or not I was out, but where I stood in relationship to what had been "promised" to me, in this case, second base.

That is the problem with living our lives with a sense of disbelief rather than belief. We don't necessarily quit following God, but we aren't doing all that we are supposed to do. The nation of Israel does the same basic thing and sits still for forty days, waiting on the spies to bring back their report about a land that has already been promised to them.

The spies sneak into the land and take note of its bounty. They even bring back produce to prove the fertility of the ground and the vast crops that can be grown. With such a good report to confirm that the land does in fact flow with "milk and honey," they are now ready to move forward, right? Wrong. God's people have another case of the "buts."

"But the people who live there are powerful, and the cities are fortified and very large," the spies report (this discussion begins in Numbers 13:28). Caleb, one of the spies, interjects, "We should go up and take possession of the land, for we can certainly do it" (Numbers 13:30).

Then the other spies jump back into the discussion. Notice the "but" contained in the scriptures: "But the men who had gone up with him said, 'We can't attack those people; they are stronger than we are.' And they spread among the Israelites a bad report about the land they had explored. They said, 'The land we explored devours those living in it. All the people we saw there are of great size. We saw the Nephilim there (the descendants of Anak come from the Nephilim). We seemed like grasshoppers in our own eyes, and we looked the same to them'" (Numbers 13:31-33).

Joshua and Caleb are the only two spies who maintain they can take the land; the others say they will be devoured if they do so. Our world needs people who live their lives this way. It needs people who take a stand and speak out when the world is heading the wrong way. The people of Israel are about to head the wrong way, and these men are determined to do all they can to rally the nation to move forward and possess what is promised.

Nonetheless, the people choose to believe the other ten spies. They now believe God cannot do what he has promised. In fact, by Numbers 14:2-4, they have this to say: "All the Israelites grumbled against Moses and Aaron, and the whole assembly said to them, 'If only we had died in Egypt! Or in this desert! Why is the LORD bringing us to this land only to let us fall by the sword? Our wives and children will be taken as plunder. Wouldn't it be better for us to go back to Egypt?' And they said to each other, 'We should choose a leader and go back to Egypt.'"

The people have done a complete about-face. They are now non-believers with no hope, instead of believers with fulfilled promises awaiting them.

In Numbers 14:21-24 God speaks, saying, "Nevertheless, as surely as I live and as surely as the glory of the LORD fills the whole earth, not one of the men who saw my glory and the miraculous signs I performed in Egypt and in the desert but who disobeyed me and tested me ten times—not one of them will ever see the land I promised on oath to their forefathers. No one who has treated me with contempt will ever see it. But because my servant Caleb has a different spirit and follows me wholeheartedly, I will bring him into the land he went to, and his descendants will inherit it."

Because they do not believe, all the people twenty years old and older wander in the wilderness for forty years. Although the land promised to them lies very near to them, they can't possess it, because they do not believe God can make good on what he has said he will do. After forty years, all these people are dead, but Joshua is alive and leads Israel on a conquest of those lands, and Caleb too is alive to make the trip. Finally, they are rewarded for their belief and for speaking out for God.

The Israelites see God's power as he delivers them from Egypt, yet they fail to recognize what he can do for them as they face this new challenge. It is easy for us to pick on these people today, as we read their story and incredulously wonder how they could lose faith so fast. But are we not equally guilty for not recognizing what God can do for us? We have the entire Bible to show us how God has interacted with his people and what he has done for them. We have example after example of fulfilled promises.

In a sense, we have something equal to the Israelites watching God work miracles to bring them out of Egypt. We have God's promises and we have no excuse to say "But..." That certainly doesn't mean we should just throw ourselves headlong into something without giving it any thought. We should pray about matters and at times seek counsel from godly people. Our next chapter speaks about answering God's call to serve him, but the first step is to live our lives in view of what he has promised us.

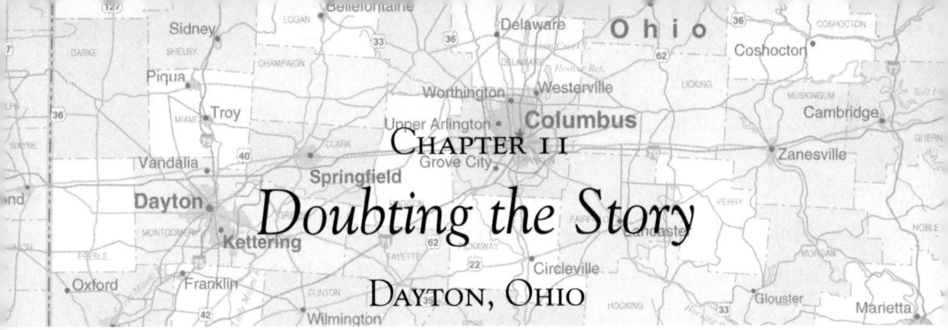

Chapter 11
Doubting the Story
Dayton, Ohio

Then he said to Thomas, "Put your finger here; see my hands. Reach out your hand and put it into my side. Stop doubting and believe." Thomas said to him, "My Lord and my God!" Then Jesus told him, "Because you have seen me, you have believed; blessed are those who have not seen and yet have believed."

—John 20:27-29

The news from Kitty Hawk, North Carolina, was hard to believe. A telegram had just arrived at the Wright family's home on December 17, 1803. The message from Orville to his parents read as follows:

```
176 C KA CS 33 Paid.                  Via Norfolk Va
Kitty Hawk N C Dec 17
Bishop M Wright
                                      7 Hawthorne St
Success four flights thursday morning all against twenty
one mile wind started from Level with engine power alone
average speed through air thirty one mile longest 57 sec-
onds inform Press home Christmas.
                                      Orevelle Wright 525P
```

The telegram contained a couple of errors, including the spelling of Orville's name and the correct length of the longest flight (59 seconds instead of 57). Yet the message proclaimed the news of the first successful flight of an airplane, a message that, ironically, few newspapers were interested in printing. Even the Wrights' hometown paper in Dayton snubbed the story as unworthy since the craft had only been in the air for 59 seconds, if in fact it had even accomplished that.

Only the telegraph operator in Kitty Hawk found the story of interest, and he relayed it to his friend, Harry P. Moore of the *Norfolk Virginian Pilot.* That paper was the first to run a story about the flight. Moore, who was not present for the flight and had only the telegraph message from which to work, began to fill in the holes with his own story. In it he wrote of a three-mile flight that traversed sand dunes and the ocean at a height of sixty feet. Of course, the story was far from correct.

If you ever have the chance to visit Kitty Hawk or Huffman Flying Field in Dayton where the brothers later developed the airplane, you should take the opportunity to learn about the years they spent making the plane into a viable machine. It is fascinating to me just how many people were skeptical of the Wrights' accomplishments each step of the way, but it's hard to blame people for doubting the story. After all, such a craft had never flown before. Unless people saw it, they had a hard time believing that men were really flying in the skies around Kitty Hawk and, later, around Dayton.

Each of us is a doubter...it's part of life. Probably no one in the Bible has been labeled as big a doubter as Thomas. Whether or not you know much about the Bible, most people have heard the expression "Doubting Thomas," the term slapped on those who for some reason don't believe the story they are told. It's unfortunate that Thomas is often made out to be a bad guy for not believing that Jesus rose again from the dead three days after his crucifixion, for he is simply expressing the feelings that many had then and now.

The Bible tells us that Jesus appeared to his disciples on Sunday evening, the same day he arose from the tomb. All of the apostles save Thomas were present, and those ten (Judas had committed suicide after betraying Christ) even doubted they were really seeing Jesus. Jesus said to them in Luke 24:38-39, "Why are you troubled, and why do doubts rise in your minds? Look at my hands and my feet. It is I myself!"

For Thomas, hearing this news may have been like hearing that an airplane carrying a man had flown through the air. Although Thomas probably respected his fellow apostles, how could he believe the story that Jesus was alive? Likewise, how could the people of the early 1900s believe the Wrights had indeed flown a heavier-than-air craft? Both needed more information to make up their minds.

I remember the last high school basketball game of my freshman year. Our varsity team was average, with about as many wins as losses. We entered the district tournament and needed a win against our rival, the best team in the conference, in order to advance further in the playoffs. They had already beaten us twice that year and neither game was close, so it was going to be a very tough task.

Spurred by the extra motivation that this could be the final game for the seniors, we played a good game, but fell one point short at the buzzer. That was it; the season was over. I can remember the final game of every one of my four basketball seasons. You don't forget those games because you know it is the last game for the seniors on the team, and eventually it will be your last game, too.

No sooner had we hit the locker room than we heard someone running down the steps, yelling for our coach. I could tell from the tone of the conversation that something exciting was happening upstairs in the gym, but I couldn't make out the words. Suddenly the coach burst into the locker room and exclaimed, "Don't take off your uniforms; the scorebooks don't agree! They say we didn't lose; the game is tied!"

You can imagine how much excitement that created as the superintendent headed back to the gym and our coach once again began drawing plays on the board that we could run in the presumed overtime period that was ahead of us. But as more and more plays were drawn on the board, no updates came from the gym. I began to wonder exactly what was happening up there.

During the coach's strategy session, our team's student manager who took care of the towels and water quietly slipped into the locker room and took a seat watching the coach draw up more plays for another five minutes. At that point, frustrated at the lack of information coming from the gym above, the coach turned to Aaron and said, "Go upstairs and find out what's going on."

Aaron didn't budge, and a sheepish grin came over his face. "The superintendent sent me down to tell you we lost by a point, so we don't need to go back to the gym."

I think our coach could have choked Aaron. There he'd sat as the coach had drawn up plays, but he'd been afraid to interrupt. Our hearts sank. It was as though we'd lost twice, once on the court and again in the locker room.

I can't imagine what it felt like for Jesus' disciples and followers to watch him be crucified on the cross. He was the Messiah, wasn't he? He was supposed to be the king. All of their hopes were gone, their time wasted. What were they to do now?

You have to wonder, as news of the resurrection spread on that Sunday, what thoughts were going through Thomas' mind. "Could this really be true? Is it not over after all? Is there really more?" Thomas had the reaction any of us might have had. He doubted.

Alfred Lloyd Tennyson wrote, "There lies more faith in honest doubt, believe me, than in half the creeds." Indeed, our doubt leads us to examine situations and serves to increase our faith far more than simply reciting a creed.

Thomas wanted to see the scars from the nails and the sword that had pierced Christ's side. He wanted the facts, and he got them a week later when he saw Jesus. Jesus said to Thomas, "Put your finger here; see my hands. Reach out your hand and put it into my side. Stop doubting and believe."

"Thomas said to him, 'My Lord and my God!'

"Then Jesus told him, 'Because you have seen me, you have believed; blessed are those who have not seen and yet have believed'" (John 20:28-29).

Can we really believe without seeing Jesus? Can we see him today? I have a children's message I enjoy presenting in which I hold a red drinking cup in front of the kids. I ask them what they believe might be in the cup. I get a variety of answers, including the response that the cup is empty.

I ask if there is any way to figure out what is in the cup without looking inside. The children soon decide to shake the cup to see if that helps. Upon shaking it, they hear the jingle of what sounds like coins inside. They are then allowed to reach a hand inside the cup, but they are still not allowed to look.

Instead of just saying there are coins inside the cup, they soon begin telling me exactly what and how many coins there are, and when we finally dump the contents out and look, they are correct.

Thomas sees Christ face to face, but we see Christ in other ways. For example, we see his creation, the beauty of the Earth that is not mere circumstance but designed by our creator. Romans 1:20 says, "For since the creation of the world God's invisible qualities—his eternal power and divine nature—have been clearly seen, being understood from what has been made, so that men are without excuse."

But there is much more. We see the changed lives of the disciples and the changed lives of believers today. We see the lives and actions of many who have faithfully followed Christ. We see the scriptures themselves that have been faithfully passed from one generation to another.

One of the greatest highlights of the radio work I have done was making a visit to Mobile, Alabama, to see an exhibit of the Dead Sea Scrolls. The scrolls contain the text of many of the Old Testament books plus other writings about the lives of those who faithfully copied and preserved these words. The scrolls were discovered in 1947 when a boy found them in a cave, where they had been hidden.

These scrolls predate the earliest known copy of the books of the Bible by about one thousand years. When scholars began to compare them to the Bible we have today, they found the words had been faithfully transmitted, that the message of old is the same message we have today! Again and again, the world around us points to God and his faithfulness toward man.

Paul writes in Hebrews 11:1, "Now faith is being sure of what we hope for and certain of what we do not see." He spends the entire chapter addressing the subject of why he believes by faith.

We are a generation that Jesus describes to Thomas when he says, "...Blessed are those who have not seen and yet have believed." Though we have not seen him face to face, our faith is not blind or without foundation. We do not have to live our lives in doubt.

Chapter 12

Trusting in Big Barns

Everett, Washington

And I'll say to myself, "You have plenty of good things laid up for many years. Take life easy; eat, drink and be merry."

—Luke 12:19

In 1966 when Boeing announced it would build the world's largest airplane, the 747, it also needed to build the world's largest structure in which to construct it. By 1968, that building was complete and the first of the giant aircraft began rolling off the assembly line. Having been present for a broadcast, I can tell you that the 747 does "roll" off the line, but it does it ever so slowly. Although multiple 747, 767, and 777 planes can be constructed at once, it usually takes around five days for one to be built.

As impressive as these giant planes are, the building they are constructed in is even more impressive to me. It's the world's largest building in terms of volume. This massive structure covers an area of 98.3 acres, with a roof eleven stories above the floor. The dimensions of the place make everything inside look like miniatures of the real thing.

In the gospel of Luke we read about a very large building of the day, a building needed for the work being done, but the motive behind its construction bears a lesson for readers today. Jesus opens the passage by telling his audience, "Watch out! Be on your guard against all kinds of greed; a man's life does not consist in the abundance of his possessions" (Luke 12:15).

He continues with this parable: "The ground of a certain rich man produced a good crop. He thought to himself, 'What shall I do? I have no place to store my crops.'

"Then he said, 'This is what I'll do. I will tear down my barns and build bigger ones, and there I will store all my grain and my goods.'" Jesus concludes this story with the man boasting, "And I'll say to myself, 'You have plenty of good things laid up for many years. Take life easy; eat, drink and be merry'" (Luke 12:16-19).

There is nothing wrong with what this man decides to do, at least in the beginning of the story. I live and work on our family's farm and we recently put up a large new grain bin. It can hold about 18,000 bushels of grain. We hadn't put up a new bin in over thirty years, so we needed more room to store our crops. There is nothing wrong with running a good business and expanding it when necessary. The problem for this man, and for any of us in our work, is what the "new barn" represents to us.

The man in the book of Luke is living to make money. He is living with the purpose of building bigger and better things to ensure his own pleasure in life. Proverbs 23:4-5 says, "Do not wear yourself out to get rich; have the wisdom to show restraint. Cast but a glance at riches, and they are gone, for they will surely sprout wings and fly off to the sky like an eagle."

We may be tempted to say, "I'm not like the farmer in the story. I don't worry about making money like he did. I don't think of my possessions in that way. Besides, I give money to help those in need." That may be true, but it is sometimes difficult for us to get a good grasp on exactly what we have. We may not be in a place to truly understand just how we have been blessed. Let me explain…

My wife lived in Bolivia for two years and still returns regularly to help with medical missions to that country. On a recent trip she was translating for a doctor who was assisting an older lady with a sore back. As Paula translated for the doctor, she asked the woman if she could perhaps put a board underneath her mattress. This would provide extra support as she slept and hopefully help relieve her aches. Upon hearing the doctor's remedy the lady replied through Paula, "I have no bed; I sleep on the floor."

We often don't have a good grasp on the blessings we have because we don't know what it's like to do without everyday luxuries. In the next chapter I talk more about our attitude toward those in need, but our outlook should first be to recognize the many blessings God has already provided for us. Many times we begin to "trust" in big barns, to place emphasis on earthly possessions, without realizing we are doing so.

When I was in first grade our class had a Christmas party and each of us brought a gift to be exchanged. A number was placed on each present and we then drew for gifts. I can still remember looking under the tree and spotting a box that was at least as twice as big as any other gift. That's the present I wanted!

We drew for numbers and that's exactly the present I got. Wow! I was so excited to see what was inside! I ripped off the paper, opened the box, and found a rubber ball attached with an elastic string to a wooden paddle.

That's not what I was expecting. I don't know what I was expecting, but that wasn't it. Not only was I disappointed by the contents of the largest box, what did I do next? I compounded my troubles by looking around the room at all the gifts from the other boxes I wished I'd received instead.

You see, when we begin to focus on the possessions of this world, we miss out on the greater gifts God gives to us. Imagine a tree laden with presents from God, but we go over to another tree and open all the lesser gifts there and never get around to opening his. In a sense, that's what the farmer was doing, and it may be what we are guilty of as well.

The parable concludes, "But God said to him, 'You fool! This very night your life will be demanded from you. Then who will get what you have prepared for yourself?'

"This is how it will be with anyone who stores up things for himself but is not rich toward God" (Luke 12:20-21).

What good is life if we store up earthly possessions but miss out on God? Consider these famous words from the same chapter: "For where your treasure is, there your heart will be also" (Luke 12:34). What are the treasures we seek? Where do we store them and with whom do we share them?

Chapter 13

"Just" a Man

Lander, Wyoming

But a Samaritan, as he traveled, came where the man was; and when he saw him, he took pity on him. He went to him and bandaged his wounds, pouring on oil and wine. Then he put the man on his own donkey, took him to an inn and took care of him.

—Luke 10:33

They say that once you leave school, you begin to learn what the "real world" is like. I remember the day after I graduated from college, my dad came to campus with our pick-up and trailer to help me pack and haul things out of my apartment. It was a hot day in late May and the trip home would take over three hours. I followed in my car and the two of us made the trip together.

We had only traveled fifty miles down the interstate when the pick-up began to overheat, and we soon figured out the truck had major problems that we wouldn't be able to fix along the side of the road. We were able to call for a tow truck that arrived over an hour later, but what I remember from the experience is sitting there along the side of that interstate packed with weekend traffic. Cars and trucks sped by, and it appeared they didn't even see us stranded along the road.

There wasn't any need for them to stop, because we had our situation under control, but I couldn't help but wonder what they would do if we really did need help. What if we had no way to signal to them yet we were in desperate need of attention?

We've all had the experience of seeing someone whose vehicle has broken down. In today's world we are sometimes afraid to help others because we might be putting ourselves in danger. This chapter isn't so much about helping stranded motorists as it is about our outlook on serving those in need.

Most of us have heard the story of the Good Samaritan in Luke 10:30-37. Jesus begins, "A man was going down from Jerusalem to Jericho, when he fell into the hands of robbers. They stripped him of his clothes, beat him and went away, leaving him half dead." It is significant to me that this man does not have a name. He isn't anybody special to those involved in the story; he is just a man going down from Jerusalem to Jericho.

The road is about twenty miles long, but very dangerous. It is a well-traveled highway of the day, yet one along which thieves often hide. Because there is regular "traffic" on the road, people passing by can see the man who is in need. A priest and a Levite both see him, but they continue on their way without stopping. They could have had a number of good reasons. They know that thieves sometimes use a decoy such as this to ambush someone who stops to help. Regardless of the reason, neither helps.

Then, one of the most unlikely characters comes to the traveler's aid. "But a Samaritan, as he traveled, came where the man was; and when he saw him, he took pity on him. He went to him and bandaged his wounds, pouring on oil and wine. Then he put the man on his own donkey, took him to an inn and took care of him. The next day he took out two silver coins and gave them to the innkeeper. 'Look after him,' he said, 'and when I return, I will reimburse you for any extra expense you may have'" (Luke 10:33-35).

There is hostility between the Samaritans and the Jews. The man lying at the side of the road could easily have been Jewish, an enemy of the Samaritan. *Easton's Illustrated Dictionary* describes the relationship of Jews and Samaritans: "After the return from the Captivity, the Jews in Jerusalem refused to allow [the Samaritans] to take part with them in rebuilding the temple, and hence sprang up an open enmity between them. They erected a rival temple on Mount Gerizim, which was, however, destroyed by a Jewish king (B.C. 130). They then built another at Shechem. The bitter enmity between the Jews and Samaritans continued in the time of our Lord: the Jews had 'no dealings with the Samaritans.'" Based on this description, the Samaritan certainly had reason to think he didn't need to stop and help.

For a few years I volunteered at a leadership camp high in the mountains above Lander, Wyoming. I really enjoyed my time there and found the camp always did a good job of challenging high school students to become difference-makers in their local communities. One year a girl showed up who, on the outside, didn't look like anything special. Perhaps I should say she was "just" a girl. Her clothes were worn, she wore thick glasses, her hair looked as if it hadn't been combed for a couple of days, and one of her shoes had a small hole in it. She was also very shy and rarely spoke to anyone.

During the first two days of camp, I often saw this girl sitting by herself in the cafeteria. Occasionally another camper would stop to visit with her, but she often remained by herself. It didn't appear she had made any new friends.

On the third day of camp, the director, Al, stood in front of the group to introduce a new counselor at the camp. "Susan has helped us for several years here at camp," he said, "but she couldn't make it up here until today because of her job. Let's welcome her back to camp." With that the students gave a nice round of applause as the new counselor walked forward to say a quick hello to the group.

"Even though I haven't been with you for the first couple of days, I still feel like I know you very well," she said. The statement seemed a little puzzling to many, especially since she did not say anything else, but simply walked to one side of the room and began rummaging through a box. From the box she pulled some old clothes and put them on over those she was wearing. She placed thick glasses on her head, messed up her hair, and put the worn-out shoes on her feet.

She had suddenly been transformed into the girl no one talked to at camp. No one had even noticed she wasn't in the room that morning. No one had missed her until now. With that, Al walked back in front of the group. "All of you want to become great leaders, but leadership starts when we work to help everyone." Nothing more needed to be said. Everyone knew how they had treated the young lady. Some had actually done a very good job of trying to befriend her. Others had not.

Jesus concludes the story of the Samaritan with, "'Which of these three do you think was a neighbor to the man who fell into the hands of robbers?'

"The expert in the law replied, 'The one who had mercy on him.'

"Jesus told him, 'Go and do likewise'" (Luke 10:36-37).

As I reflect on these stories and think about my own life, I am reminded of how little I sometimes do to help others. Perhaps each one of us can say this. Jesus challenges each of us to think about who is our "neighbor." He challenges us to reach out to everyone everywhere. Everyone is someone special to Him; we are never "just" a person to God.

In Matthew 5:43-48 Jesus has this to say about our relationship with others: "You have heard that it was said, 'Love your neighbor and hate your enemy.' But I tell you: Love your enemies and pray for those who persecute you, that you may be sons of your Father in heaven. He causes his sun to rise on the evil and the good, and sends rain on the righteous and the unrighteous. If you love those who love you, what reward will you get? Are not even the tax collectors doing that? And if you greet only your brothers, what are you doing more than others? Do not even pagans do that? Be perfect, therefore, as your heavenly Father is perfect."

The story of the Good Samaritan is one of the best-known stories from the Bible, yet we may struggle with its application. Jesus asks of us to "go and do likewise." It is a principle we should remember each day.

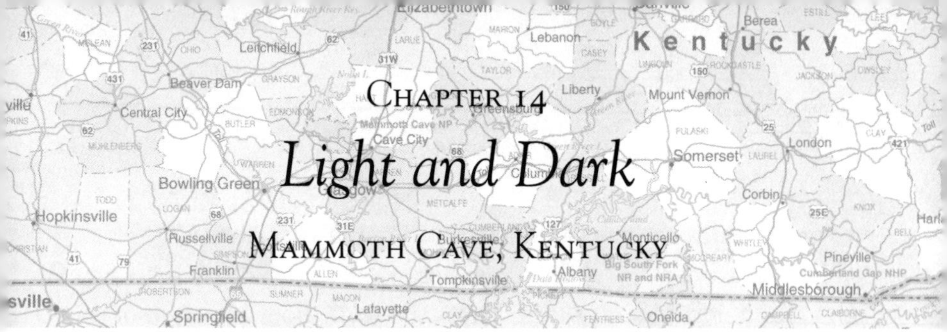

Chapter 14
Light and Dark
Mammoth Cave, Kentucky

Light has come into the world, but men loved darkness instead of light because their deeds were evil.

—John 3:19

Over my lifetime I have visited lots of caves. For some reason I never get tired of heading underground to look at the stalagmites and stalactites and to experience a totally different world. On one trip to Kentucky, I visited Mammoth Cave National Park, the longest cave system in the world, with 360 miles explored and mapped. Although I was there to conduct radio interviews, I also went on a tour of the cave.

I have toured enough caves across the nation to know there is a staple of almost every single tour, and no matter how many times I witness it, I am still amazed. There comes a point when the guide, such as mine at Mammoth Cave, will say, "To show you just how dark it is in a cave, I'm going to turn out the lights." This is the staple you can always expect, but there was one extra caveat on this day.

"I've got some matches," our guide added, "and when all of the lights are out, I'll strike one so you can see just how much light one flame can make in this cave." With matches in one hand he turned out the lights with the other. I could hear him take the match and strike it against the box, but there was no spark and no flame. In addition, I heard the box of matches fall out of his hands and onto the floor of the cave. "Uh oh," his voice uttered from the pitch black. "Hold on a second…I'll find them here somewhere." With that came the sound of his hands sifting across the rocky floor in search of the matches.

We were never in danger of being left in the dark, but this situation did make me wonder how a person would find his way out of a cave without any light. The answer is, he wouldn't. There is nothing as dark as the inside of a cave. No light can enter. Even on a cloudy, moonless night above ground, you can still see your hand in front of your face, but in a cave, you can see nothing.

The Bible contains plenty of imagery of light and darkness. The book of John opens with a discussion of Christ as the light of the world: "Through him all things were made; without him nothing was made that has been made. In him was life, and that life was the light of men. The light shines in the darkness, but the darkness has not understood it.

"There came a man who was sent from God; his name was John. He came as a witness to testify concerning that light, so that through him all men might believe. He himself was not the light; he came only as a witness to the light. The true light that gives light to every man was coming into the world" (1:3-9).

Christ is described as the light of the world. John the Baptist came to "witness" and "testify" of him, declaring that Christ was the "true light that gives light to every man." Just as a match is struck inside a dark cave, Christ's light leads us out of the darkness. Although Christ's light shows a clear path out of the shadows, we have a problem: we often prefer that some of what we do remain concealed in the dark.

Christ speaks of the battle between light and dark. He describes himself as the "light" in John 3:19-21, saying, "Light has come into the world, but men loved darkness instead of light because their deeds were evil. Everyone who does evil hates the light, and will not come into the light for fear that his deeds will be exposed. But whoever lives by the truth comes into the light, so that it may be seen plainly that what he has done has been done through God."

On a visit to Timpanogos Cave National Monument in Utah, I interviewed a guide about this small cave that is often listed as one of the toughest to visit because of a one-and-a half mile hike up a steep trail in the mountains to reach it. The guide turned off the lights and we discussed just how dark it is in a cave. He said, "People just don't understand what darkness is. They tell me, 'Oh I'm sure my eyes will adjust if I just spend enough time in here in the dark.' But they won't. There's no light here. Your eyes can't adjust when there's no light."

Yet, many times we live our lives believing we can find some light in a place that is totally dark. Listen to the words of 1 John 1:5-9 and what it says about darkness and light: "God is light; in him there is no darkness at all. If we claim to have fellowship with him yet walk in the darkness, we lie and do not live by the truth. But if we walk in the light, as he is in the light, we have fellowship with one another, and the blood of Jesus, his Son, purifies us from all sin. If we claim to be without sin, we deceive ourselves and the truth is not in us. If we confess our sins, he is faithful and just and will forgive us our sins and purify us from all unrighteousness."

We often choose darkness over light because of sin in our lives. Darkness provides a cover for deeds we'd rather not have anyone else see. Yet, God does see; he has the perfect view of our lives. In fact, in the next chapter, I discuss how light illuminates even things we don't want seen. Are our lives filled with sins we hope darkness will hide, or do we live lives that shine in the light?

When I fly, which is pretty often, I always try to get a window seat. I love geography and am very good at figuring out where we are based on the landmarks, even when we are high above the ground.

At night I can usually spot airports with ease. That's because there is a spot where the street and house lights stop, leaving a dark void in the city. There is usually only one way I know that what I am seeing is an airport rather than an empty space. This is the beacon, the bright shaft of light that spins round and round. This is proof to me that an airport exists below. Christ's light is likewise a beacon for our lives, guiding the paths we should follow.

Christ describes himself as light: "I am the light of the world. Whoever follows me will never walk in darkness, but will have the light of life" (John 8:12). Christ is the "light of life." God's words direct our way. "Your word is a lamp to my feet and a light for my path" (Psalm 119:105).

In the last chapter of the Bible, we are told that heaven itself is full of light: "There will be no more night. They will not need the light of a lamp or the light of the sun, for the Lord God will give them light. And they will reign for ever and ever" (Revelation 22:5).

Are we living our lives in the light?

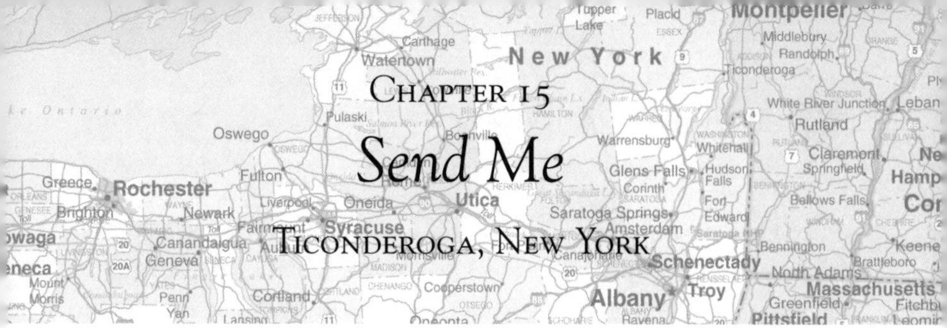

Chapter 15

Send Me

Ticonderoga, New York

Then I heard the voice of the Lord saying, "Whom shall I send? And who will go for us?" And I said, "Here I am. Send me!"

—Isaiah 6:8

Although we today know Benedict Arnold as a traitor, there was a time when he was an American hero in the fight for freedom. It was on the night of May 10, 1775, that Arnold, along with another patriot hero, Ethan Allen and his Green Mountain Boys, led a surprise attack against the British at Fort Ticonderoga. The two men caught the British soldiers totally unawares and took control of the fort without a shot being fired.

If you go to Fort Ticonderoga today, you will find a beautifully restored fort with a commanding view of the southern reaches of Lake Champlain. You might also be surprised to learn the story of Ethan Allen. While we know that Benedict Arnold later switched sides and became one of the best-known traitors in history, few know what happened to Allen. Most history books tell of his heroic capture of Fort Ticonderoga, but that is where the story ends. We'll get back to that piece of history in just a moment.

In Isaiah 6, the death of King Uzziah is recorded. 2 Kings 15:3 tells us that Uzziah "did what was right in the eyes of the LORD" and that he reigned for fifty-two years. Some Bible scholars believe Uzziah is the last "good" king the southern kingdom of Judah has. After his death, subsequent kings don't seek to serve God, the kingdom begins to deteriorate, and many people are taken captive by neighboring nations.

Isaiah knows that things are not headed in the right direction for his country, and it is at this time that God calls him to service. Isaiah sees a vision of God in his glory and writes, "I saw the Lord seated on a throne, high and exalted, and the train of his robe filled the temple. Above him were seraphs, each with six wings: with two wings they covered their faces, with two they covered their feet, and with two they were flying. And they were calling to one another: 'Holy, holy, holy is the LORD Almighty; the whole earth is full of his glory.' At the sound of their voices the doorposts and thresholds shook and the temple was filled with smoke" (Isaiah 6:1-3).

Isaiah's reaction is interesting. His words speak to something we may not think about too much today. "'Woe to me!' I cried. 'I am ruined! For I am a man of unclean lips, and I live among a people of unclean lips, and my eyes have seen the King, the LORD Almighty.' Then one of the seraphs flew to me with a live coal in his hand, which he had taken with tongs from the altar. With it he touched my mouth and said, 'See, this has touched your lips; your guilt is taken away and your sin atoned for'" (Isaiah 6:5-7).

When men see God's glory in the Bible, they are struck not only by God's power and righteousness; they see just how unrighteous they are in comparison. This is true for Daniel and Paul (Saul on the road to Damascus) and Isaiah in this passage. Isaiah calls himself "unclean" and unworthy to be found in God's presence.

I once took a ride in a state highway patrol helicopter that is used for search and rescue missions as well as manhunts (no, I was not under arrest). Two pieces of equipment fascinated me. One was an extremely powerful searchlight. The pilot said he could illuminate an entire football field bright enough to play a game with that one light. In fact, the light was so bright that it had a device that would not let it swivel too close to the body of the helicopter. If the light hit the shell of the craft, it would burn the paint right off the metal.

The other feature was a special heat-sensing camera. Even on a pitch-black night, the camera could see animals and humans hiding in the woods as clear as though it were day. Even if a convict escaped in the middle of the night, this camera would still be able to see the fugitive.

God is light. He sees all our sins. We can't cover them with darkness. Isaiah knows that if God is going to use him, he needs to make himself clean. He needs to purge the sinfulness from his life. Isaiah does two things that are important for us today: he reveres God's majesty and he confesses and repents of the sin in his life. He knows he needs to be in a right position with God in order to be useful to Him: "Then I heard the voice of the Lord saying, 'Whom shall I send? And who will go for us?' And I said, 'Here I am. Send me!'" (Isaiah 6:8). God is asking for someone to carry his message to his people. He is looking for a godly person to fill the role.

I believe God does the same thing today. He is looking for people to fill roles in service to Him. He needs people committed to living godly lives who will respond as Isaiah did.

Ethan Allen was the type of man who seemed very useful to the patriot cause. He was a daring leader who led men to capture a vital fort. But there is something else we need to know about Allen. Upon taking command of Fort Ticonderoga, Allen and his men got drunk on the liquor inside for three days. One writer describes him as an "overbearing, loud-mouthed braggart." Another says, "An awful infidel, one of the wickedest Men that ever walked this guilty globe." Not long after taking the fort, Allen and his men made a poorly designed attempt to take the city of Montreal. The British captured Allen and held him for most of the rest of the Revolution.

While I was doing broadcasts in the area, I asked one guide at the fort about Allen's life in captivity. She told me, "Normally exchanges would take place between captured British and American officers. But Washington was very afraid of Ethan Allen…he was a 'loose cannon,' and Washington decided it would be better to keep him in prison rather than to exchange him." Although Allen really wanted to be back on the field of battle, other areas of his life prevented him from being a trusted leader. He could not serve his new country until he cleaned up other areas of his life.

God wants to use us in service to him. He is looking for people who will call out just as Isaiah did, "Here I am. Send me!" We, as Isaiah, need to shine a light on our lives and see the areas that hold sin, things that keep us from living lives fully devoted to God. We need to come to God in reverence and in sincere repentance for our sins. God uses Isaiah as a mighty voice in a time of despair. He can use each of us to do great things as well.

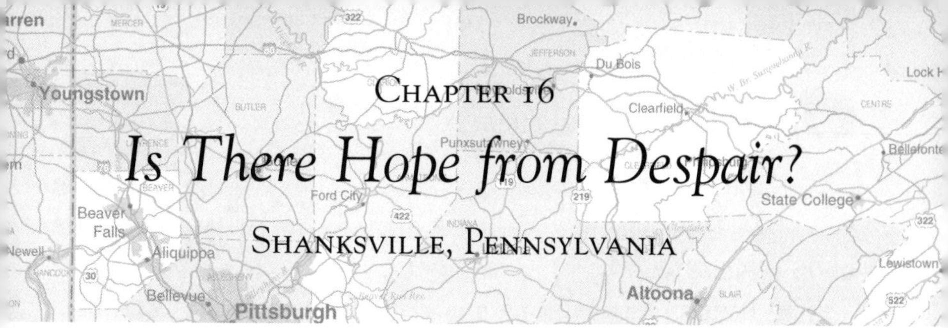

CHAPTER 16

Is There Hope from Despair?

SHANKSVILLE, PENNSYLVANIA

Naked I came from my mother's womb, and naked I will depart.
The LORD gave and the LORD has taken away;
may the name of the LORD be praised.

—JOB 1:21

My work in radio has always involved writing features. These are usually pieces that highlight interesting places and people in the nation and around the world. If I cover a sad or tragic story, it is usually years later, as I share a story of triumph out of despair.

A couple of years after the September 11 tragedy, I was in Shanksville, Pennsylvania, to share the story of the memorial being built to commemorate the heroism of the passengers who battled with hijackers for control of United flight 93. These passengers ultimately saved the lives of others when they gave their own. Their story is one that still brings tears to my eyes as I contemplate "ordinary" Americans making an extraordinary sacrifice.

While in Shanksville, I noticed a story that you may have heard as well. It is the type of story that I find again and again when I cover the aftermath of tragic events years later. The story was first reported in the local newspaper in Johnstown, Pennsylvania, a story of a Bible from flight 93. Rescue workers reported "no pieces bigger than a dinner plate" were found at the crash site. Only two items larger than that description were in fact found, a tire from the landing gear and an open Bible.

The Bible rested a few yards from the impact crater and was lying open. One firefighter said, "There definitely was a feeling that God's hand was present. The leather cover on the Bible was singed, but none of the pages were burned. It was an older Bible that you could tell was used a lot."

Reverend Joe Maurizio, a local Roman Catholic priest, said, "In my own personal opinion, this is a miracle and a sign from God that while the things that we have can all be destroyed, the Word will never die. And God's love for us will never pass."

Sometimes in the middle of despair, Jesus answers us so loudly. Some may believe this story is just a coincidence, yet I've reported stories about similar instances many times. This story is not really about a Bible that survived a crash, but instead about a God who wants us to know that while we sometimes can't understand difficult times, he is still in control and still loves us.

How can a tragedy have anything close to a happy ending? As I stood next to my grandfather Saunders' hospital bed, I wondered why such a wonderful Christian man had to endure a two-month battle with cancer. He could no longer communicate with our family and it was difficult to even visit him. Why would God let something like this happen, especially to someone who had proclaimed God's goodness and faithfully lived a Christian life? Why, God? Why?

Some might believe my grandfather had a right to be angry with God, yet that's not the way he felt. Why didn't he? Why shouldn't he have been mad at God? The reason is that my grandfather believed Christ had given much more.

Think about it. If anyone ever had a reason to ask, "Why do bad things happen to good people?" it was Christ. He was sinless, totally innocent, yet he endured a painful death on a cross. What my grandfather realized was that Christ endured death to take the sins of the world upon himself. Christ went to the cross in order that all men and women might have life for eternity through Him. When we keep this in mind, it changes our perspective on difficult times.

Consider that in the first two chapters of the book of Job, Job loses all of his oxen, donkeys, sheep, and camels. Many of his servants are killed. All of Job's sons and daughters die. To top it off, Job is stricken with disease and sores.

What does Job say? "Naked I came from my mother's womb, and naked I will depart. The LORD gave and the LORD has taken away; may the name of the LORD be praised" (Job 1:21). Job knows God is his creator and he trusts in Him. God is in control. God will provide for him.

In times of tragedy, we no doubt feel sorrow and pain. We may search for meaning but find little. Our frustration might make us begin to question our actions. Is there something we could have done differently? Could this be punishment for something we did? Jesus explains in Luke 13:3-5 that "bad" events are not metered out proportionally when one has done wrong. We, like Job, probably never discover why such events happen. However, like Job, we are called to trust in God. In fact, Job's great faithfulness to God even through difficult times is later rewarded. You can read about it in the last chapter of Job.

No, we do not always understand why certain difficult events happen in our lives, but we shouldn't think God hands out disaster at will, that he randomly brings difficult events to pass. Romans 8:28 says, "In all things God works for the good of those who love him, who have been called according to his purpose." In Romans 8:31 Paul goes on to state, "If God is for us, who can be against us?"

God never leaves us. As the famous "Footprints" poem depicts, in times of our deepest pain, when we see but one set of footprints in the sand instead of two, these are the times that Christ carries us. Talk to God and ask for strength and understanding at these times, realizing that Christ is there to "carry" us through them (Psalm 23).

In 1994 one of my closest friends unexpectedly died. He was someone I worked with and someone who had become a great friend to our family. I flew home from a trip to South Dakota to be a pallbearer at his funeral. Sometimes when I go to his grave, I wonder "Why…Why?" Sometimes I wish I could see things from God's viewpoint.

The night after my friend's funeral I went to a Kansas City Royals baseball game. It may sound insensitive, but some of my greatest thinking has been done while sitting in that ballpark. 1994 was a difficult year for the Royals as their Hall of Fame hero, George Brett, had retired the year before. Now the team was looking for a new hero, someone to step forward and lead the team.

That night I saw a pitchers' duel as Kansas City trailed 1-0 in the bottom of the ninth. Then, with a runner on first base, a rookie by the name of Bob Hamelin stepped to the plate. On that hot summer night, the team was struggling. Not only had they not scored a run, they were in need of someone who could fill the role of Brett, who often came to the plate to help the team win a big game.

I remember the moment so well. Bob Hamelin drove that fastball high and deep to right field. From my seat down the right field line that night, I was so close I could see the seams on the ball as it flew high above me. I can still see that ball clearing the fence, bouncing in the bullpen with fireworks booming into the sky. Bob Hamelin circled the bases as his team ran to greet him at home plate. He drove in two runs with one swing and quickly ended the game in the Royals' favor.

As I drove home that night, tears ran down my cheeks. I realized that going to that game was what I'd needed to do. My friend who had just passed away was so important to me. He had been a vital part of our business. Even at a time of total loss, a time of void, God has called you and I not to sit on the bench. We have seen the wonderful example provided by the heroes before us. We are called to keep going and to keep relying on God in our times of deepest need. We pay tribute to the lives of those we love through the actions of our own lives.

"Forgetting what is behind and straining toward what is ahead, I press on toward the goal to win the prize for which God has called me heavenward in Christ Jesus" (Philippians 3:13-14). No, we will not forget those who have set the example, but we must press forward. We must get off the bench. We must not simply watch Christian heroes but carry on with the tasks they have begun.

As I stood atop a hill next to my grandfather's casket the day before Thanksgiving in 1998, tears filled my eyes. "Why should I be thankful?" I wondered. Then I remembered, "Where, O death, is your victory? Where, O death, is your sting?" (I Corinthians 15:55). Death does not triumph over a believer in Christ!

I'm told that my grandfather's favorite verses in the Bible were Philippians 4:8-9: "Finally, brothers, whatever is true, whatever is noble, whatever is right, whatever is pure, whatever is lovely, whatever is admirable—if anything is excellent or praiseworthy—think about such things. Whatever you have learned or received or heard from me, or seen in me—put it into practice. And the God of peace will be with you."

Granddad used to add, "If you think about those things, you'll do a lot less thinking about any problems you believe you have."

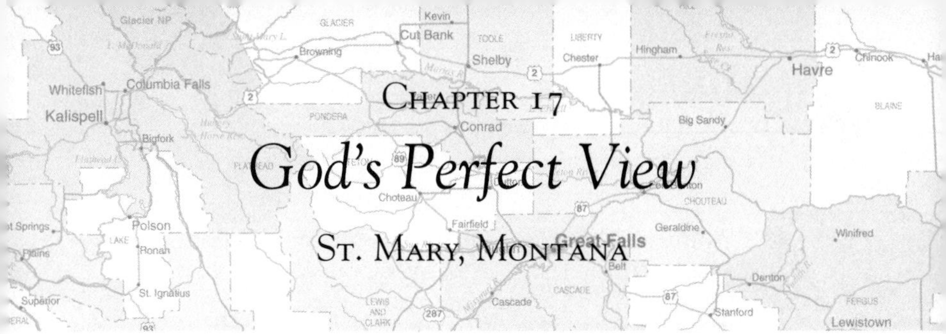

Chapter 17

God's Perfect View

St. Mary, Montana

I am your brother Joseph, the one you sold into Egypt! And now, do not be distressed and do not be angry with yourselves for selling me here, because it was to save lives that God sent me ahead of you.

—Genesis 45:4-5

"How much farther ya think you guys can go?" I panted to my friends, hands on my knees, staring at the worn rocky path at my feet. It wasn't as if we were about to die, yet I didn't know if we could physically manage what was still ahead of us. Three of our friends had already turned back, and now only four of us remained.

"We could save a lot of time if this thing went straight to the top," panted Greg, referring to the trail that seemed to go everywhere except where we wanted it to, which was to the top of Triple Divide Peak, the point where the Continental Divide and the Hudson Bay Divide meet. This peak, towering 8,011 feet above the valleys of Glacier National Park, marks the point where water either flows west to the Pacific, north to Hudson Bay, or east and south toward the Gulf of Mexico.

We'd been on the trail now for about four hours, and although we'd made good time, we were hindered by a trail that seemed to meander through the woods and then above the tree line in its ascent of the rocky pinnacle. There were several factors to consider. Not only were we tired, if we didn't reach the summit soon, there would not be enough daylight to find our way back to camp that evening. This wasn't a life and death decision like hikers make on trips up Mt. Everest, but it was still a big one for us.

We decided to continue, the four of us climbing about ten steps, then stopping to catch a breath of thin air before moving another ten steps. Finally, the summit was in reach, but there was a surprise for us as we turned around to see the route from which we had just come…

Sometimes we hear people say things like, "Don't be sad; it's God's will" or "It's God's will for me to do this." Such statements may be true, but they can be dangerous. Sometimes people may simply slap on the title of "God's will" to justify all kinds of events or actions. The Bible does tell us several things about God's will. For instance, II Peter 3:9 says that God does not want us to perish eternally but desires each of us to repent of our sins and accept his son Jesus as savior. The Bible also teaches that it is God's will for us to study his word and to live a life filled with his Spirit.

God's will applies to all of us, and God's plan includes the specific steps he wants us to take to serve him. I've often wondered, how do I know if I am living God's plan? How do I know if I am living or moving in the direction God wants for me? How do I know what job to take, whom to marry, where to live, where to go to church, or how God wants me to serve him? How should I react when doing the right thing seems to result in failure?

Sometimes we do not get the view we want. Sometimes we must accept that we don't know why God has allowed certain events to unfold. In our ascent up Triple Divide Peak, my friends and I experienced several frustrating things. Not only was the path difficult and steep, the route did not seem to make sense. We could see our goal, yet we appeared to be moving in directions that were not the most practical way to reach the peak.

Most of us could probably say the same thing for many aspects of our lives. We may have a good idea of what we would like, but it seems we are either not headed there or at least not headed that way very quickly.

The important point to remember is that God always has the best view. Isaiah 55:9 notes, "As the heavens are higher than the earth, so are my ways higher than your ways and my thoughts than your thoughts." We must accept that when viewing life, God has the perfect view of the field from the blimp hovering over the stadium. He gets to see all the events at once, from the beginning of time to the end of time. Though it's nice that God can see everything, if we can see nothing, we are often left frustrated, still looking for direction.

Romans 8:28 may be one of the most comforting verses in the Bible when we begin to wonder about God's plan for our lives. It says, "And we know that in all things God works for the good of those who love him, who have been called according to his purpose." We can be assured that if we have placed our trust in Christ and are seeking to live in his example, he is working his perfect plan in us.

But we also have a duty to be actively living for Him. We can't just sit around and expect God to work his plan. I can't just sit around and wait for someone to haul me to the top of Triple Divide Peak. It's kind of like the story a pastor once told me about the man who prayed every night that he would win the lottery, and in return he would give a big portion of his winnings to the church. He prayed this prayer day after day, month after month, year after year. One night he finally prayed angrily to God, "God why won't you grant my prayer; why won't you provide me the money to give to your church?"

To his surprise, God's voice boomed out, "Why don't you help me out and buy a lottery ticket?"

Have you "helped God out"? Have you made a commitment to pray to Him about your direction in life? Have you committed yourself to living according to his word? Are you seeking to live close to Him?

We also must remember that we are supposed to live God's plan, not ours. Romans 8:28 says "his" purpose, not "our" purpose. That purpose may come at lighting quick speed or it may come after what seems a great delay. We can't get caught praying the prayer, "God grant me patience and I want it NOW!"

One of the most beautiful passages in the Bible that demonstrates God's perfect plan is found in the book of Genesis. It is a story that begins in Genesis 37 and continues for several chapters and it concerns the life of a man named Joseph. Joseph is one of twelve sons born to Jacob, but of those twelve, Joseph is Jacob's favorite.

Joseph's eleven brothers resent the fact that Jacob shows favoritism toward Joseph. Their bitter feelings finally lead them to capture their brother and sell him as a slave to the members of a caravan heading to Egypt.

To cover up their evil deed, Joseph's brothers tell their father that Joseph has been killed by a wild animal. They produce Joseph's coat, which they have soaked in blood, as evidence of his death. For Jacob and the remaining sons, that seems to be the end of the story, but of course it isn't.

Joseph is taken to Egypt by the caravan that has purchased him as a servant of Potiphar, a captain in the Egyptian army. Joseph does his job well and Potiphar makes him ruler of his household. There is only one problem: Potiphar's wife likes Joseph. She likes him so much that she wants to have an affair with him. Joseph knows this is wrong, for he is a man who follows God. He knows that while Potiphar's wife is tempting, having an affair with her would be contrary to God's will.

But why should Joseph care about that? God has given him a rotten deal, hasn't he? Joseph has been sold by his own brothers and is now a slave in a land far from home. Despite that, he has risen to a chief position in Potiphar's house...a position whose power can only increase by having an affair with Potiphar's wife. **No one but the two of them would ever know, plus she would put in a good word for Joseph and make sure he always got the best of everything. God would surely understand why it would be all right to do this, wouldn't he?**

Think carefully about those bolded words. Our situation may not be identical to Joseph's, but there are many times when we choose to do wrong and even try to justify it. Joseph indeed gets a rotten deal when he is sold into slavery, but he doesn't abandon his faith. He doesn't know where God's path is going to lead, but he isn't going to leave the path.

Joseph consequently refuses to sleep with his boss's wife. He could have rationalized doing so in many different ways, but he won't turn from how God wants him to live. When Potiphar's wife sees that Joseph will not commit this sin, she falsely accuses him. She tells her husband that Joseph has tried to rape her. Instead of having everything he could ever seem to want for doing wrong, Joseph is thrown into jail for doing what is right.

Nonetheless, doing the right thing is never wrong, though it sometimes takes a while for us to see why following God is so important.

Time passes. Pharaoh has a troubling dream that no one can interpret. Since Joseph has been interpreting dreams for some of the king's staff while in jail, they recommend his services to the king and he is brought to Pharaoh. With God's help, he interprets Pharaoh's dreams and predicts seven years of great crops in the land of Egypt followed by seven years of famine. Pharaoh is so amazed that he makes

Joseph second in command. What a promotion...from prisoner to vice president in a matter of seconds!

The famine eventually strikes all of Egypt and the surrounding nations, and Joseph's father and eleven brothers are affected. In their despair, ten of the brothers travel to Egypt in search of food. They wind up in front of their brother asking to buy food, but they have no reason to suspect he would be in such a position and they don't recognize him. Though Joseph recognizes them, he does not reveal his identity.

Eventually all eleven of Joseph's brothers travel to Egypt to buy food from Joseph. Now, with all of his brothers standing in front of him, Joseph can't control his emotions. He has seen God's plan revealed. In Genesis 45:4-5 he says, "I am your brother Joseph, the one you sold into Egypt! And now, do not be distressed and do not be angry with yourselves for selling me here, because it was to save lives that God sent me ahead of you."

What a beautiful picture! Joseph could have been livid! His brothers have sold him as a slave! He has been accused of attempted rape! He has been forgotten in prison! For a while, it seems that doing the right thing only gets him deeper and deeper into trouble. Notice that doing God's will, making decisions that are pleasing to God, seems to move Joseph in the wrong direction. But in the end, God's plan comes together. God's timing places Joseph in a position to save his own family by providing them the food they need to survive the famine.

You see, God has a lot better view than you or I. He can see how all the twists and turns in the trail are going to get us to where we need to be. I must admit that many times in my life, I have felt like I am in the middle of a dense forest in the dark. I can't see why God has put me in such a terrible place. Why has he seemingly placed such pain in my life? Why has he closed this door? Why do others seem to be moving ahead while I have been forgotten? Why God, why?

When Jesus dies on the cross, it must seem that God has brought something extremely positive to an end. Little do the disciples know that in three days, they will see God's plan. They will see the resurrection of Jesus. They will see why his path has sent him to a painful death on a cross.

...As my friends and I took the last difficult steps to the summit of Triple Divide Peak, for the first time we turned around to see our view. Wow! We were well above the tree line. We could see into Canada and deep into central Montana. We could see the trail so far below weaving among the trees and rocks. We could even see small lakes partly covered with ice due to the high altitude. The four of us sat down and didn't say a word, partly because we were out of breath, and just stared at what our hike had produced.

It was then that I finally saw the path we had taken. It was unmistakable as it wove among the trees, crossed streams, and then made the few long switchbacks to the top. For the first time, I saw why the path couldn't have been straight. There were numerous obstacles to avoid. To lay out the path differently would never have brought us to this point.

As I look at my life, I can see many wonderful things that God has done. I can also see times of despair and worry, times when I made a wrong turn, times when I wondered why God had shut a certain door, times when I wondered why a company didn't hire me or why someone I was dating decided to dump me. All of us have felt the pain of loneliness. We have all felt times when God has seemed far away and oblivious to us. But once in a while, we see one of those beautiful scenes from high above, a view of how God has used both "good" and "bad" events to bring us to where we need to be. He is able to do that when he keeps our sights on serving Him.

The company Reality Living published a workbook on God's will that reads, "Be what he wants you to be, and He will show you what to do." I won't tell you that "being what he wants you to be" will always win you immediate fame and fortune, but I will tell you that "all things work together for them that love God."

Someday, we will each look back and get a glimpse of the wonderful scenery behind us and see that God's perfect plan has led us to where we need to be. That is truly something beautiful.

Chapter 18

The Coonskin Example

Amesville, Ohio

And the things you have heard me say in the presence of many witnesses entrust to reliable men who will also be qualified to teach others.

—II Timothy 2:2

I was struggling in school; there was no doubt about that. Although I was working hard to master the material, extra effort did not produce improved results. My mom and dad had certainly tried to help me, but with every source seemingly exhausted, my granddad was called in. After all, he was accomplished in the area, and maybe the grandfatherly approach would be just the thing to help me understand what was before me.

I remember the day I went to my grandparents' house and sat down at the kitchen table with Granddad. He had been briefed and was ready to help. He smiled at me as we sat down at the kitchen table together and said, "So Andrew, they tell me you're having trouble learning to tie your shoes."

Yes, I was lagging behind in kindergarten because I simply couldn't tie my shoelaces. Granddad and I spent most of the morning working on the pattern again and again, his seventy-five-year-old hands patiently helping my small fingers make the loops and ties to keep the shoes on my feet.

Teachers play a very important role in our lives. These teachers can be people who help us in a literal classroom, but they are also family members, friends, and even individuals we meet just once in our lives. Every minute can be a teaching and learning moment as we observe what is around us.

II Timothy says much about teaching others. That book, which is a letter written by Paul to Timothy, is the last recorded letter we have from Paul. In fact, the words contained within it seem to indicate that Paul knows his time here on Earth is drawing to a close. The book is one of my favorites, as it serves as spiritual motivation from the mentor Paul to his "student" and fellow evangelist Timothy.

Paul recalls Timothy's faith and writes, "I have been reminded of your sincere faith, which first lived in your grandmother Lois and in your mother Eunice and, I am persuaded, now lives in you also" (II Timothy 1:5). This is but one verse in the Bible, but it is a verse that speaks volumes about young Timothy.

Who are Lois and Eunice? They are mentioned by name just once in the Bible, but the fact that their names appear one time does not mean they aren't important. They are Timothy's mother and grandmother, and they represent first-generation followers of Christ. These two ladies have a tremendous impact on their son and grandson, a subject discussed by Paul and even the gospel writer Luke. In fact, Luke refers to the women in Acts 16:1.

Early Christians knew one of the factors behind Timothy's zeal to serve and share was the teaching of his mother and grandmother, who knew the importance of raising Timothy in a home where the scriptures were taught.

Like Timothy, our experiences as children greatly influence our adult lives. I once traveled to tiny Amesville, Ohio, a town in the southeastern part of the Buckeye state, that once was home to the "Coonskin Library." In the early nineteenth century, settlers there desired to educate themselves and learn more about a variety of subjects. To do that, they needed books, so they formed their own library association and set dues at $2.50. In 1804, Samuel Brown took

$73.50 to Boston, where he bought the first fifty-one books for the new library.

One of the youngest members of the library association was Thomas Ewing, a teenager who paid his dues with his winter hunt of coonskins. His sister taught him to read, and after working long days on the farm, he often devoted his nights to reading. He later described the feeling of having books in his frontier town, stating, "It seemed to me like an almost unbounded intellectual treasure…The library of the Vatican, and all other libraries of which I had read, were trifles, playthings, compared to it."

The example Ewing saw in his family and community inspired him to become an avid reader and a good student. He was one of the first graduates of the University of Ohio and later became a United States senator from Ohio, secretary of the treasury under Presidents William Henry Harrison and John Tyler, and secretary of the interior under Presidents Zachary Taylor and Millard Fillmore. During one of Ewing's political debates, his challenger made a belittling remark: "All Ewing knows is what he read in that coonskin library." The title stuck, and the library that educated Amesville and the well-known Ewing was forever after known as the "Coonskin Library."

Just imagine: reading and education were so important to the people of Amesville that they saved their money and went all the way to Boston to get books. Thomas Ewing benefited from the work his parents and others did to fund that library. His life was a product of what he learned as a child. In much the same way, the book of Timothy shows that Timothy's life is a product of what his mother and grandmother teach him as a child.

I once interviewed the mother of a well-known NASCAR driver about what it was like to have a famous son involved in an exhilarating yet very dangerous sport. It was a fun talk, and two points still stand out in my mind. One, she told me how she and her son used to race on dirt tracks in Kentucky and that she even beat him on a few occasions! Two, she told me she always had a way to talk to someone in her son's pit crew if there was a problem during a race. Prayer was a very important part of her life and her son's, and her love for him meant she always had a way to check on him if something went wrong in a race.

Obviously, this woman influenced her son's love for racing, and her role as a loving and concerned mother never ceased. Timothy's mother and grandmother were just the same. You have to wonder if Eunice ever said something like, "Now Timothy, you be careful when you're around Paul and try not to get hurt." She probably knew that Timothy was going to endure hardships spreading the gospel message, but she also knew she had taught him love for Christ.

You may have noticed that this book is dedicated to a couple of Sunday School teachers. My family and many others have been great influences on my spiritual life, but I wanted to thank these two ladies in particular because they volunteered their time as teachers to work with kids. Each of us is an example and influence to others, and that influence begins at birth. We can be teachers within our family or influencers in our community, but make no mistake about it, our actions always affect someone.

Paul knows this. He urges Timothy, "But as for you, continue in what you have learned and have become convinced of, because you know those from whom you learned it, and how from infancy you have known the holy Scriptures, which are able to make you wise for salvation through faith in Christ Jesus" (II Timothy 3:14-15). When does Timothy's education begin? In infancy.

I wonder if Paul may have been a little jealous. Remember, Paul takes up the cause of Christ after a miraculous conversion on the road to Damascus (Acts 9). He doesn't have a family to teach him what he now shares with others. Paul wants Timothy's life to be something all can have. He shares, "And the things you have heard me say in the presence of many witnesses entrust to reliable men who will also be qualified to teach others" (II Timothy 2:2). In other words, don't break the chain. Whether they are your children, family, friends, or even strangers you meet only once, be prepared to teach.

We are an example one hundred percent of the time. I don't get the feeling that Timothy went to church once a month and that was the extent of his Christian upbringing. The values, the scriptures, every aspect of the world around him, influenced his future. Timothy becomes an evangelist, but regardless of the path of our lives, this continuous influence is vital. There is a definition for leadership that states, "Leadership is influence." That means each of us is a leader, because each one of us influences others. How are we influencing the lives of those around us?

Timothy is told by Paul not to forget what he has been taught in his youth. I remember being proficient in solving quadratic equations in high school, but I would be hard pressed to solve them now. Why? Because I don't practice solving quadratic equations today! Similarly, how can we expect to grow spiritually if we don't take the time to continually learn and grow?

Failure to transmit vital information from one generation to the next can have negative consequences. Consider this: after the fall of the Roman Empire, the "recipe" for making cement seems to have been lost, so cement was not used in the dark ages until it was rediscovered centuries later. Knowing how to make cement is important in building things, but somewhere the chain was broken and the recipe had to be relearned. For a long time, society suffered because it lacked a way to make cement. In much the same way, Paul urges Timothy and other readers not to neglect the sharing of the gospel message in their families and communities.

I should pause to share a quick story about how we might be tempted to think we've failed to share and thus have broken the chain when in reality we have not. After a speaking engagement one day, a lady approached me and told me she wanted to speak with me when I had a free moment. About ten minutes later, I stepped into the foyer and she shared with me that her son was in prison for using drugs. She wondered if I might pray for him. She hoped that God might somehow speak to him inside that cell and that he would begin to turn his life in a new direction.

She told me, "He was raised in a Christian home and went to church every week. He was baptized in the church, too. I think God will use him to reach others who've abused drugs someday. We want to see him, but he denies our request and says it's too far for us to have to drive."

I think about that family and still pray for that young man. His mother loved him dearly and had done everything she could to guide him like Eunice and Lois had Timothy. Sometimes individuals take a wrong turn and do things that are out of our control. But remember, if the seed has been planted, hopefully that individual will return to what was once learned. Pray about the situation, but don't feel you are a failure.

Maybe you will be the first link in a chain. You might be in the role of Paul, a man who turns his life around to become a follower of Christ and then lives to teach others. Whatever the story of our lives to this point, Paul's message to us is relevant today.

In this last letter to Timothy, Paul challenges, "You then, my son, be strong in the grace that is in Christ Jesus. And the things you have heard me say in the presence of many witnesses entrust to reliable men who will also be qualified to teach others" (II Timothy 2:1-2).

We are part of a chain. Whether we are the first link in the chain or several links down the line, our job is to do what Timothy is charged to do, to share the gospel that is able to "make you wise for salvation through faith in Christ Jesus" (II Timothy 3:15).

My granddad lived on the farm to the age of ninety-five and then had to move to a nursing home where he lived to just a couple of weeks shy of his ninety-eighth birthday. On one of those final visits to see him, I was on a special mission: he'd requested I go to the store and pick something up for him. He had few wants, so I knew this had to be important.

I went to his closet as he lay resting on his bed and retrieved the shoes he wore around the home. As I pulled up a chair next to his bed, I carefully took the worn laces out of his shoes and replaced them with the new laces I had just purchased. I carefully put each shoe on his foot, and as I finished tying his shoes, I remembered...the man who had taught me to tie my shoes now needed me to tie his. What he'd taught me, I now did for him.

What we have been taught about living for Christ, I hope we will each share as well.

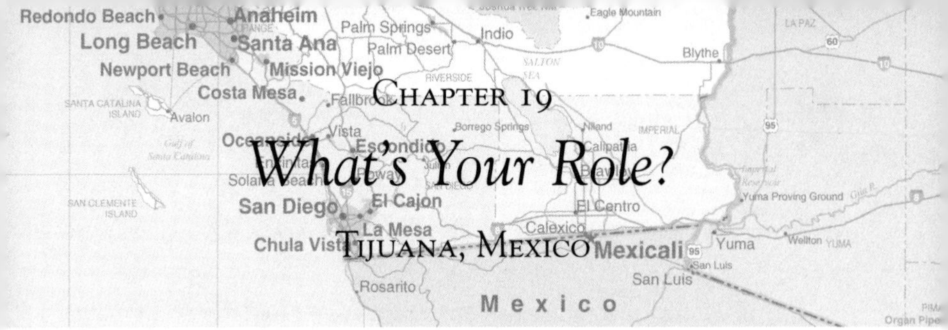

Chapter 19

What's Your Role?

Tijuana, Mexico

Then Mary took about a pint of pure nard, an expensive perfume; she poured it on Jesus' feet and wiped his feet with her hair. And the house was filled with the fragrance of the perfume.

—John 12:3

I will never forget the summer of 1988, working the dusty farm fields around our home, watching as corn plants curled and soybeans withered with a relentless string of one hundred-degree days that slowly choked the life from the crops. So little rain had fallen in the two months since the seed had gone into the ground that you could still see the tracks the planter had made as it went through the field that spring.

It was one summer afternoon during that drought that my dad came to the hay field where I was working and announced that we had "an important visitor" coming to see the farm the next day. The state was so dry that the governor himself was touring the area and we had been called to host one of his stops. That was big news! We immediately began to do what we could to prepare not only for the governor but also for the press who were traveling with him.

I will always remember riding in the back of a pick-up, me a teenager, visiting with the governor about just how dry it was on the farm and how it impacted our livelihood. The governor really seemed to respect my opinion, and I guess he should have since I had been in the fields working just like everyone else.

John Ashcroft was governor at the time, and he later went on to become the nation's attorney general, a prominent role in the months and years following the September 11 tragedy. I laugh to think that he once spent an afternoon riding around in the back of our dusty pick-up. It seems such a small matter in comparison to fighting terrorism.

Probably each one of us has had times when we've hosted someone "important" at our home or business. Maybe we took extra time to make our place look nice to impress the guest. I remember once being on an important business visit to the president of a very large bank. Our team of six had a few minutes in the board room before the president came in to meet with us, and in just those few minutes, our team's leader quickly told each of us where to sit. He positioned certain people closer to the president, depending on what their role was during the meeting.

In John 12, three siblings, Lazarus, Martha, and Mary, have differing roles as they prepare for an important visitor, Jesus. Not only had he been a guest in their home before, his last visit produced a miracle when he raised Lazarus from the dead (John 11). Even though the family knows Jesus, we see that they still go to great lengths to make him feel at home. It is the role that each of the three people in that home fill that speaks to us today.

Lazarus' role is simply to sit at the table to eat and visit with Jesus. That may not sound like a big job, but it certainly was important. How can a guest feel welcomed if they don't have someone with whom to talk? Today, people all around us are looking for someone with whom to visit. Perhaps a person in a nursing home would love to have a visitor or a neighbor down the street would like someone to enjoy a cup of coffee with. Such small acts shouldn't be overlooked, because they aren't small at all. They are important, and it is this role that Lazarus fulfills in his meal with Jesus.

This meal takes place just a week before Jesus is crucified, and some believe Lazarus is raised from the dead just a couple of months before the meal they now eat. In fact, later in this chapter, we are told that the chief priests are making plans to put Lazarus to death as well as Jesus, since Jesus' miracle in bringing him back to life is causing even more people to begin following Jesus.

Martha also plays an important role in this story, for without her, there would have been no meal to eat. We are simply told that she "served." You might be surprised at the little things you and I can do to help serve. In several years of speaking to groups, I've learned that one of the biggest things I can do to serve is to help set up the meeting room. If I walk into a room and people are still setting up folding chairs and tables, I usually try to jump in and assist. People are really grateful when the speaker himself helps them get the place ready. I try to always remember that something as small as setting up folding chairs can be a form of service. There are plenty of ways around us to serve.

It's Mary's role in this meal that gets the most notoriety. What does she have to offer? Lazarus is already eating and talking with Jesus, and her sister Martha is serving the meal. Maybe Mary can assist one of them, but there seems to be nothing of her own to offer. We see in a moment that not only does she find a way to serve, what she does is still an example to us today.

There probably never has been a journey that taught me as much about filling our unique roles as the recent trip I made across the border south of San Diego to Tijuana, Mexico. A team of about fifteen people was headed into the border city to visit an orphanage and assist with medical check-ups for the kids there. I was a little nervous about helping out, not because I didn't want to be of service, but because I didn't know any Spanish and I had never been to this orphanage before. I really wondered if I had any skills to offer.

Soon I felt like the equivalent of the last kid picked when dividing teams on the playground. I just didn't have anything to offer. Everyone else was really good at something, but I excelled at nothing. Five medical doctors were working with our group, and how I wished I were a doctor. I didn't even speak Spanish, so I was no use as a translator. What on earth was I going to do?

"Andrew, I've got a job for you," said the leader of the trip as she finished assisting one of the doctors with setting up his exam area.

"What do you have for me?" I replied, expecting it to be some aspect of helping the doctor.

"I'm going to take you over to the room where all the boys at the orphanage stay. You can keep them entertained before they have to come visit the doctor," she replied.

My heart sank. "Keep them entertained?" I thought to myself. I sure was vital to the trip, wasn't I? If ever there was something that said, "You're unimportant," it was to be asked to keep kids entertained.

We walked across a small courtyard to a plain, unpainted door, behind which I could hear the screams of what seemed to be a playground full of children, except for the fact that all the noise was coming from inside the room instead of outside. What could be behind that door? Exactly how many kids were there?

"The orphanage has about fifteen three- to eight-year-old boys. They'll be glad to see you. There's only one girl to look after all of them." With that the leader opened the door to what instantly became a mad rush of children climbing on top of me. Within two seconds I had children swinging from my arms and attached to my legs. As one fell off an arm, another jumped on, and other kids climbed to the top of their bunk beds for a chance to leap onto my back. I was a morsel of food under attack by a swarm of ants determined to devour me!

One thing I quickly learned is that you don't need to know much Spanish to entertain a group of kids in a Mexican orphanage. I also learned that nothing will wear you out more quickly than trying to keep an entire orphanage entertained before the "scary" trip to the doctor. When I emerged from the room three hours later, I appeared to have done battle with a pack of wolves.

I was later told that the role I played that day might have been the most important of all to those boys. While the medical check-ups were vital in assuring their health and the translators were needed to relay that information to the children and supervisors, the staff at the orphanage was so small that it was rare an adult had time to play games with the boys. In addition, the staff was entirely female, so it had been a long time since a male was there to entertain those boys, a role I filled that day.

We are sometimes tempted to feel we have nothing to offer, yet we have so much to share in a multitude of ways. Mary didn't fill the role of either Lazarus or Martha, but she, too, had much to give. John 12:3 records, "Then Mary took about a pint of pure nard, an expensive perfume; she poured it on Jesus' feet and wiped his feet with her hair. And the house was filled with the fragrance of the perfume" (John 12:3).

This was not any ordinary perfume or ointment; this was *very* expensive stuff. It might have cost as much as a year's wages for an average person, and it might have been purchased for Mary's own burial someday.

Stop and think about that for a moment. On what would you be willing to spend your entire year's salary? Mary spends it to honor Christ. She knows that his time on Earth is drawing to a close, and she even uses her own hair to wipe his feet, an act of service and humility.

Judas objects to what takes place, questioning whether the money should be given to the poor instead. Giving to the poor is certainly a good thing to do, but Judas does not have a benevolent heart. We are told that he is a thief and that this is money he might have used for his own desires. We have a contrast here between Mary with her sacrificial giving and Judas with his self-centered heart, a heart that will betray Jesus later that week.

My wife spent two full years in Bolivia serving as a volunteer with a program through her church. She still volunteers there during the summer as a translator on medical missions to the country. On her first trip to the small town in which she spends much of her time, she saw a little girl playing in the street. The girl wore a pretty necklace that appeared to be homemade. Paula stopped and complimented the girl on the beautiful necklace she wore. The girl stopped, reached behind her neck and unclasped the chain, and with an outstretched hand, offered it to her.

That's the kind of heart Mary has. The Bible shows us she is a person willing to give all she has to help another. I am always amazed that people who have the least seem willing to give the most. Lazarus, Martha, and Mary have hearts that are ready to serve and give. They each have a role, and each role is important in serving Christ.

What role can each of us play in our service to Him?

Chapter 20

We'll Never Say Good-bye

King City, Missouri

He will wipe every tear from their eyes.
There will be no more death or mourning or crying or pain,
for the old order of things has passed away.

—Revelation 21:4

I was the only one home when my grandfather McCrea passed away. My parents happened to be away from the farm on a much-deserved vacation when he unexpectedly died. It was a Sunday morning when I got the call, and I remember heading to the funeral home to begin making the arrangements.

It was weeks later that I heard an interesting story about my grandfather from one of the nurses at the home where he resided. I have known her all my life, as she is the mother of one of my best friends. She said, "You know, the day before your grandfather passed, I was taking care of him in his room and he said something interesting to me. He told me, 'I see angels.'" She went on to tell me that this was not the first time she had heard something like that from a resident. As she spoke, it occurred to me that my grandfather was seeing the angels sent to carry him home.

You see, this book is about the very subject with which we began…foundations. Our journey has led us right back to the little basement with the craggy wall with all the Bible stories pictured upon it. It leads me back to my family, friends, and others who provided me a Christian home in which to live and grow. But now the work falls to you and I, first to build our own lives upon the correct foundation, and second, to raise up another generation who will also make Christ the foundation of their lives.

In the last letter the apostle Paul writes to Timothy, shortly before his death, Paul encourages Christians, "And the things you have heard me say in the presence of many witnesses entrust to reliable men who will also be qualified to teach others" (2 Timothy 2:2-3). Paul teaches Timothy, who is urged to teach others, who in turn share their faith with still another generation.

Hymn number 502 is still listed on the hymn board in my living room, a reminder of the mission to share God's words with others and to make them a part of my everyday life. Though I didn't mention it earlier, my old hometown church did sing one more verse before the final service was completed that last day before the church permanently shut its doors. This short stanza was a tradition that concluded each and every Sunday service. It went,

We'll never say goodbye in glory,
in the morning over yonder.
No we'll never say good-bye in glory
no we'll never say good-bye up there!

With that, the pastor would smile and say, "I'll see you next week, or I'll see you on the way up [to heaven]!" This was a nice little way to remind us that, as Christians, we never really say good-bye.

I have a good friend who has endured some tough times in her life. When we first met, we occasionally wrote letters to one another just to share how things were going at school (this was before the days of e-mail). At the time, I didn't realize the weight of the challenges she felt, doubts that led her to consider whether life here on Earth was really worth living. I unknowingly was writing an occasional letter that gave her a lift and helped her get back on the right track. It wasn't until a couple of years after my first letter that I learned of the impact my writing had upon her.

Of course, she taught me a lot as well, including the difference kind words and encouragement can make in someone's life. I often retell her story when I speak. During a recent e-mail conversation, I told her that I would be sharing her story with another audience the next day. Upon hearing this, she asked if I would share a few more of her words to my audience. She said, "Tell them that friendships can last...and hard times don't last forever."

In many ways, that's the message of Christ. His love for us never ends. No matter what we may have done in life up to this point, he wants to enter in and have a relationship with us. In Revelation 3:20 Christ says, "Here I am! I stand at the door and knock. If anyone hears my voice and opens the door, I will come in and eat with him, and he with me." Our commitment by faith in service to him means that hard times won't last forever. God has prepared something far better for us.

Being a Christian means we never say good-bye. Although there will be a day when you and I depart this earth, we will be reunited with the many faithful followers who have gone before us. Revelation 21:4 says of heaven, "He will wipe every tear from their eyes. There will be no more death or mourning or crying or pain, for the old order of things has passed away."

I look forward to that day and I hope you do, too...a day when the followers of Christ go home to be with Him.

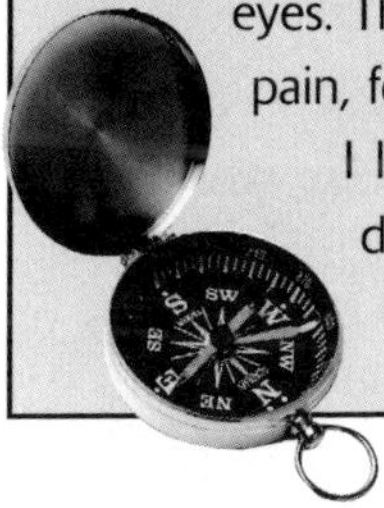